THE PIANO
CAN
BE FUN

THE PIANO CAN BE FUN

Harry Junkin & Cyril Ornadel

Based on the ATV Television Series

STANLEY PAUL
LONDON

STANLEY PAUL & CO LTD
3 Fitzroy Square, London W1

AN IMPRINT OF THE HUTCHINSON GROUP

London Melbourne Sydney Auckland
Wellington Johannesburg Cape Town
and agencies throughout the world

First published 1973

This book has been set in Baskerville and designed by Design Practitioners Sevenoaks
Printed in Great Britain on Croxley Offset paper by The Stellar Press, Hatfield,
and bound by William Brendon, Tiptree, Essex

(Cased) ISBN 0 09 115200 3
(Paper) ISBN 0 09 115201 1

Contents

Introduction

Lesson 1: White Notes   1

Lesson 2: Black Notes   11

Lesson 3: Reading of Music—Right Hand   20

Lesson 4: Reading of Music—Left Hand   31

Lesson 5: Time and Notes   43

Lesson 6: Rhythm and Rests   58

Lesson 7: Pedalling and Phrasing   67

Lesson 8: Interpretation and Shape   82

Glossary of Terms   97

Scales and Arpeggios   101

Introduction

We do not pretend for one moment that this book is in any way a definitive work on the art of piano playing. It is designed for amateurs only and we use the word in its nicest and truest sense; an amateur is somebody who cultivates something as a pleasurable pastime. The critics love to use the word amateur derisively as the only and ghastly alternative to professionalism. Well forget the critics!

Sad to relate there aren't too many amateur pianists around these days. Adult ones that is. There are amateur cricketers, footballers and bridge players but not many amateur pianists. The majority of pianists seem to fall into one of two categories.

Category one is the unfortunate youngster who starts piano lessons because his parents insist. He is bored to distraction, refuses to practise regularly and after half a thousand household rows his parents decide to spend their money on something that will either be useful or appreciated. The student rapturously says goodbye for ever to his teacher and frequently never again derives the slightest pleasure out of making any kind of music.

Category two is the terribly serious young student who works his head off until he is twenty-five and then realizes he just hasn't got what it takes to be a "great artist". He may make a living as an un-known professional musician; he might become a teacher who bores the kids in category one to distraction; but his attitude to music remains jaundiced for the rest of his life.

We believe there is a category between these two—*you*. So cultivate whatever ability you have for piano playing for the sheer fun of it. If you play a piece badly and thoroughly enjoy it whose business is it but yours? The pseudo-intellectuals of this world still try to make believe there are certain definable academic standards that must be met in order for an artist to be considered valuable. This is pretentious nonsense. You are valuable to *yourself*.

You are never, *ever*, going to give a piano recital in the Festival Hall. You know it, we know it, everybody knows it. There are too many piano recitals given in the Festival Hall anyway.

So relax, enjoy yourself, and learn, because the piano can be fun!

Harry W Junkin.
Cyril Ornadel.

Lesson 1:
WHITE NOTES

Please do not feel that because you might POSSIBLY be over eighteen years old that your days as a student are over. They are not! Most intelligent adults learn more rapidly than adolescents because they work harder and concentrate better. And the time to start learning about music or anything else is when YOU want to. It is never too late to start and it is always too early to give up.

This book is designed to avoid like the plague the stuffy, dull old-fashioned approach to the teaching of music in general and the piano in particular. God only knows how many of today's adults have been put off music for life because of having been exposed, as kids, to pompous, dictatorial, aggressive and neurotic piano teachers. It would be nice to be able to say that today such teachers are a vanished breed. But sadly they are not. You can prove this by doing a little survey of ten year-old piano students.

For all musicians who either sing, or play an instrument, the door to musical knowledge is unlocked by one key. Middle C on the piano. The piano is world-wide musical headquarters.

Pianos are made in two styles, the upright and the grand. In an upright the stringing is vertical to the keyboard. In a grand it is horizontal to the keyboard. Usually, all things being equal, a grand piano is preferable to an upright but a standard-sized upright is usually preferable to what is known as a "baby" grand. If you are considering the purchase of a piano remember that it is easy to get stuck with a lemon. A high quality piano has a life of many many years provided it has been well taken care of and regularly tuned. So don't hesitate to buy second-hand. Use the same procedure you would use if you were buying a car. It is wise to purchase a reputable and well-known make and at the same time to remember that the highly polished finish can conceal a multitude of defects. Ring up a good piano tuner and offer him a fiver to examine your piano before you buy it. An ounce of prevention is worth five pounds.

A few facts and definitions:

The Piano
is a very commonly encountered stringed percussion instrument which, in the cultured home of today, has been largely replaced by two other very commonly encountered musical instruments—the radio and the record player. Playing a piano takes more skill than playing a radio or a record player which you presumably know; otherwise you would not have bought this book.

1

Method of Playing the Piano

One or more keys are struck simultaneously or non-simultaneously, usually with the fingers but conceivably with knuckles, toes, fists or elbows. Striking the keys causes the strings to vibrate. These vibrations produce tones which may or may not be music.

The difference between you and the world's greatest pianist is purely one of degree. Once you can play Middle C you can call yourself a pianist with complete justification. The great pianist strikes the notes (invariably with the fingers) and equally invariably with vastly more skill and talent than you do.

So upwards and onwards ... El Al ... here we go!

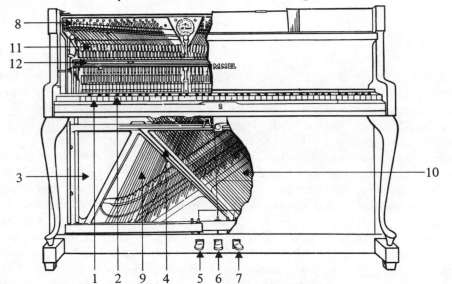

Plate 1

1 **WHITE KEYS**
You strike them as tastefully as possible

2 **BLACK KEYS**
Ditto

3 **SOUNDING BOARD**
Of wood .. which amplifies and enriches the tone.

4 **FULL IRON FRAME**
Supports the strings at high tension.

5 **SOFT PEDAL**
Moves all the felt hammers closer to the strings so that in travelling a shorter distance they produce a softer tone. On a grand piano, the soft pedal moves the keyboard action to one side so that the hammers instead of striking three strings (loudly) strike two strings (softly).

6 **SOSTENUTO PEDAL**
Don't worry if your piano hasn't one. Lots of pianos don't. When depressed this pedal keeps a single tone sustained by holding up the felt damper.

7 **SUSTAINING PEDAL**
Incorrectly called the "loud" pedal. This lifts all the dampers from all the keys and thus sustains and enriches the tone. Hold it down too long you get a pudding.

8 **TUNING PINS**
Turn these and you alter the tension (pitch) of the strings.

9 **TREBLE STRINGS**   10 **BASS STRINGS**

11 **FELT HAMMERS**
Which strike the strings.

12 **DAMPERS**
Felt faced .. pressed against the strings they keep them from vibrating.

2

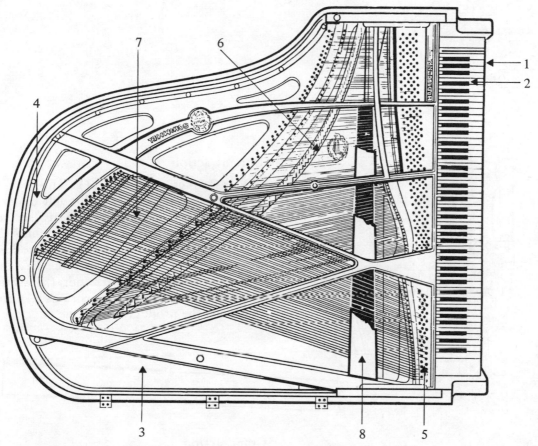

Plate 2

1 WHITE KEYS
You strike them as tastefully as possible

2 BLACK KEYS
Ditto

3 SOUNDING BOARD
Of wood . . which amplifies and enriches the tone.

4 FULL IRON FRAME
Supports the strings at high tension.

5 TUNING PINS
Turn these and you alter the tension (pitch) of the strings.

6 TREBLE STRINGS

7 BASS STRINGS

8 DAMPERS
Felt faced . . pressed against the strings they keep them from vibrating.

Felt hammers, which strike the strings, are hidden behind the dampers in this drawing; they can be clearly seen in plate 4.

NOTE: Pedal positions are exactly the same as on an upright piano—see plate 1.

3

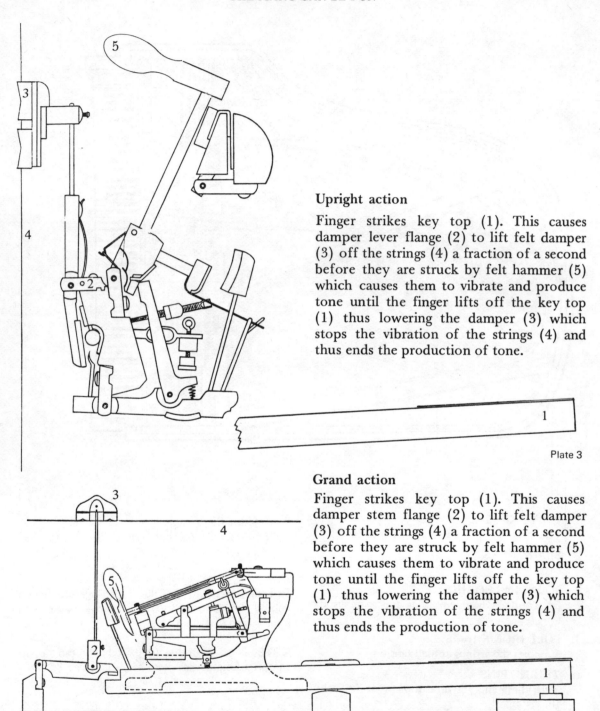

Upright action

Finger strikes key top (1). This causes damper lever flange (2) to lift felt damper (3) off the strings (4) a fraction of a second before they are struck by felt hammer (5) which causes them to vibrate and produce tone until the finger lifts off the key top (1) thus lowering the damper (3) which stops the vibration of the strings (4) and thus ends the production of tone.

Plate 3

Grand action

Finger strikes key top (1). This causes damper stem flange (2) to lift felt damper (3) off the strings (4) a fraction of a second before they are struck by felt hammer (5) which causes them to vibrate and produce tone until the finger lifts off the key top (1) thus lowering the damper (3) which stops the vibration of the strings (4) and thus ends the production of tone.

Drawn by C. Astell, Herrburger Brooks.
Reproduced from 'The Pianoforte' by W.L. Sumner. Publisher Macdonald.

Plate 4

First . . .

Know your instrument

There are many requirements of a good piano action but the most important are:

Sensitivity—so that the strength of the blow on the key top is reflected in the intensity and volume of the tone produced. The lighter the weight of the finger, the softer the tone. The heavier the weight of the finger, the louder the tone.

The felt hammer (5) must strike the string smartly and then instantly recoil from it even though the player keeps the keytop (1) depressed. Otherwise the hammer acts as a damper.

The damper (3) must instantly return to the strings (4) and stifle their vibrations when the key top pressure ceases. This permits the very rapid repetition of the note should the player be in a repetitive mood.

The sustaining pedal must instantly lift or lower the dampers (3) without making a sound.

The soft pedal must instantly shift the action without making a sound, so that no clicks or clacks intrude on the music.

It is a complicated and highly ingenious piece of mechanical engineering.

The first thing we'd like you to do is sit down at your piano in such a way that the dead centre of your body (navel) is directly opposite the centre of the keyboard. Now take a long long look at the keyboard. What you are seeing is this:

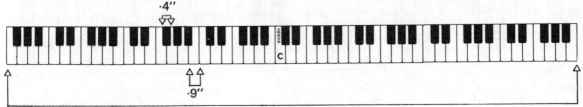

Plate 5

The standard keyboard is approximately four feet wide from the lowest note on the extreme left to the highest note on the extreme right. Most standard pianos have a total of 88 black and white notes. If your piano has one or two more or less it doesn't matter. The width of a white key is .9 inch, the width of a black key is .4 inch.

Notice that the black notes are arranged in alternating groups of two and three . . . two and three . . . two and three . . . right the way up the keyboard. There may be an extra black note on its own at your extreme left but forget about this for the moment. Please look at this grouping of black notes for a full two minutes and fix it firmly in your mind. Two black . . . three black . . . two black . . . three black . . . to the top of the keyboard.

Now look carefully at Plate 6.

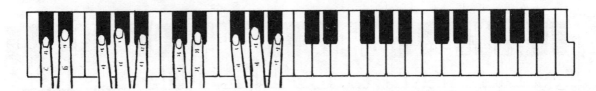

Plate 6

Play the lowest group (extreme left) of two black notes as indicated in Plate 6. Then play the next group of three black notes, then the next group of two .. and so on .. until you get to the top (extreme right) of your keyboard. As you play these notes say out loud .. two black .. three black .. two black .. three black .. etc.

Please repeat this twenty times, keeping your eyes firmly on the keyboard.

And here a comment about your attitude. Learning to play the piano should be what the verb suggests: "play". It can be play if you approach it in the right way. Remember that learning to play is really learning to practise. Solid accomplishment is never dead easy.

Grasping the physical positional relationship between the notes is the elementary first step in your getting a basic visual picture of the keyboard.

Now we're going to leave the black notes for a moment and concentrate on the white ones because the black notes all get their names from the white ones anyway, and this first lesson is solely concerned with teaching you to find and name all the white notes on your piano.

Now we would like you to pay particular attention to a group of two black notes which, if you are sitting opposite the centre of your keyboard, should be dead under your nose.

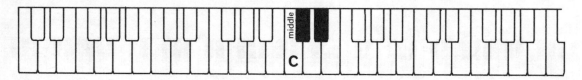

Plate 7

Now by far the most important note on your piano, or on anybody else's piano for that matter, is the white note just below and immediately to the left of those two centre black notes.

It is called Middle C.

Please practise looking away from your keyboard .. at some object in your room . . . then looking back at your key-

board and quickly picking out Middle C. Try this fifteen times. Then try moving away from your keyboard, then returning, and playing Middle C quickly. Please play and say Middle C twenty times.

Now take another long look at the whole keyboard .. paying special attention to the groups of two black notes. The white note immediately to the left .. just below each group of two black notes .. is always C. Look hard at Plate 8.

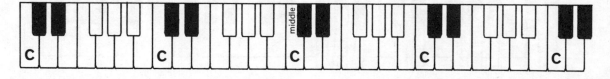

Plate 8

6

Please study this chart for a full three minutes. Fix it firmly in your mind that the white note immediately to the left and just below every group of two black notes is called C. The note below the two centre black notes is called **MIDDLE C** . . because it is in the middle of the keyboard.

Please start at the bottom C (extreme left) of your keyboard and play every C moving up (to the right). Say the letter C out loud as you play the note. C . . . C . . . C . . .

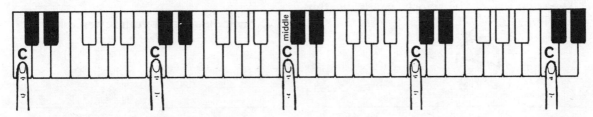

Plate 9

Then move down (left) on your keyboard playing every C.

Then practise playing "C"'s at random . . . for five minutes.

Then go away and have a drink or a cup of tea or a breath of fresh air for ten minutes.

Marking Keys

You can do this with a pencil, as soft as possible, which will rub off with a wet rag. Do not use ink or magic marker as these may stain the keys permanently. Another way of marking the keys is to cut paper into little strips a half-inch long and a quarter-inch wide . . and letter each one like this.

Plate 10

Next tear off sellotape into strips a little wider than the paper and stick these to your piano keys.

Now look at your own keyboard and say the following sentences out loud:

The white note immediately above and to the right of Middle C is D. (*MARK IT*)

The white note immediately above and to the right of D . . . is E. (*MARK IT*)

The white note immediately above and to the right of E is F. (*MARK IT*)

The white note immediately above and to the right of F is G. (*MARK IT*)

The white note immediately above and to the right of G is A. (*NOT H* as you might think. Just accept this.)

The white note immediately above and to the right of A is B. (*MARK IT*)

The white note immediately above and to the right of B is C. (*MARK IT*)

We're now back where we started. Your keyboard should now look like this:

Plate 11

7

Now look at your keyboard for a long, long moment. What we want you to do is pick out some visual positional relationships quickly. To illustrate what we're after:

You can look at a clock face that has no numbers on it . . and instantly tell the time. When you see the clock hands in this position . . .

you instantly realise that the long hand is at 12 and the short hand is at 3 and that it is three o'clock. In the same way that you don't need numbers on the clock to tell the time, you soon won't need letters on the keys to grasp their positional relationship.

Now look again at your lettered keys.

Plate 12

Here are some facts which you must make so much a part of your thinking that they become automatic, almost instinctive.

Relationships

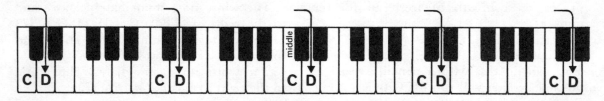

Plate 13

D The white note in the middle of each group of two black notes is always D.

Play and say all the D's on your piano ten times. Then pick out D's at random . . as fast as you can.

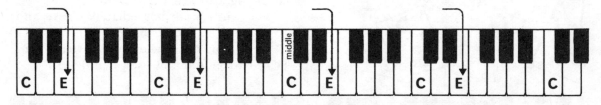

Plate 14

E The white note immediately above (to the right of) each group of two black notes is always E.

Play and say all the E's on your piano ten times.
Then pick out E's at random as fast as you can.

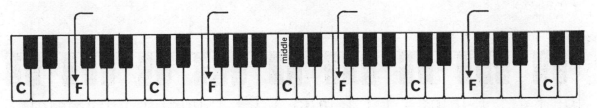

Plate 15

F The white note immediately below (to the left of) each group of three black notes is always F.

Play and say all the F's on your piano ten times.
Then pick out F's at random as fast as you can.

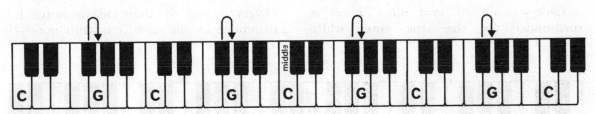

Plate 16

G The white note immediately above (to the right of) the first black note in each group of three is always G.

Play and say all the G's on your piano ten times.
Then pick out G's at random as fast as you can.

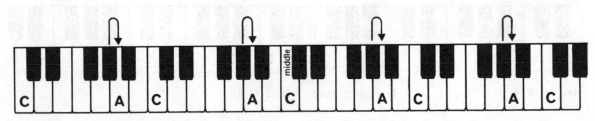

Plate 17

A The white note immediately above (to the right of) the *second* black note in each group of three is always A.

Play and say all the A's on your piano ten times.
Then pick out A's at random as fast as you can.

9

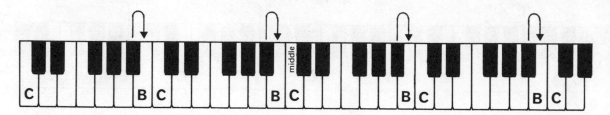

Plate 18

B The white note immediately above (to the right of) the *third* black note in each group of three is always B.

Play and say all the B's on your piano ten times.
Then pick out B's at random as fast as you can.

Every group of two black notes is surrounded by the same three white notes—C.D.E.

Every group of three black notes is surrounded by the same four white notes—F.G.A.B.

Plate 19

You now know the names of all the white notes on your piano. Practise and play and say these relationships over and over again. Have somebody help you by calling out notes at random. See how quickly you can find them.

Now to learn a piece.

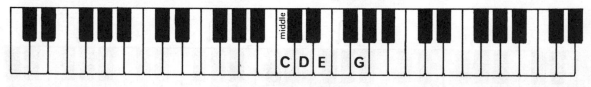

play: **E E E** and pause   **E E E** and pause   **E G C D E**   Plate 20

JINGLE BELLS
PLAY: E   THREE TIMES AND PAUSE.
PLAY: E   THREE MORE TIMES AND
             PAUSE.
PLAY: E. G. C. D. E. . . . EVENLY

You may not quite be ready for a guest appearance with the London Symphony but you've made a start and played a piece.
Congratulations! And so endeth the first lesson . . . WHITE NOTES.

10

Lesson 2:
BLACK NOTES

It is now pretty generally conceded that the first pianoforte was made by a man named Bartolomeo Cristofori, a Paduan harpsichord maker who was instrument custodian to the Medicis. The Medicis were a noble Italian family with pots of money and they could afford such things as "instrument custodians". There aren't any "instrument custodians" today—so why not appoint yourself "instrument custodian" around your pad as it has a very aristocratic ring to it. Anyway, Cristofori made the first pianoforte around 1720 and it looks very much like a grand piano of today.

The first public performance on a piano in England is thought to have taken place on May 16th, 1767, at Covent Garden. It seems that after Act I of THE BEGGAR'S OPERA, so that the audience wouldn't have a second's relaxation, somebody named Miss Brickler sang a song and was accompanied by a Mr. Dibdin on a new instrument called the pianoforte. (Piano is Italian for soft. Forte is Italian for loud.) Whether Mr. Dibdin should be blamed we don't know but the new instrument took a while to catch on. It encountered more than the usual amount of suspicion of anything "new-fangled". Let's face it there are people around today who think computers are a passing fad. Anyway, Mozart, so we are told, was delighted with it even though he had been trained and taught on the harpsichord. Incidentally the main difference between a harpsichord and a piano is that harpsichord strings are plucked with a plectrum and piano strings are struck with a felt hammer.

A few facts and definitions
A staff is a group of people who work for you, or a pole from which a flag is flown or the gnomon of a sundial. But in music a STAFF is:

a set of five horizontal lines enclosing four spaces. Musical notes are placed on the lines or in the spaces in such a way as to indicate their pitch above or below Middle C. Notes above Middle C are usually played with the right hand and notes below Middle C are usually played with the left hand.

SEMI is: Latin for half. ½! We believe that the use of Latin in the teaching of music or any other subject is somewhat pretentious and makes the subject needlessly difficult. We prefer half-yearly to semi-annually and certainly we prefer "a half pint of bitter" to "a semi-pint of bitter". Imagine how you'd react to a recipe that told you to place a semi-teaspoonful of salt in a semi-cup of water!

You are perfectly free, however, to use the word semi-tone if you prefer it. "Semi" is used pretty well throughout Europe. "Half" is used throughout North America. We shall use both.

A SEMI-(HALF) TONE is the distance up or down between any key (white or black) and the next key (white or black) to it.

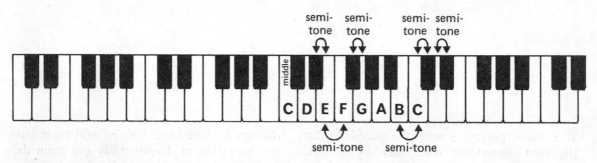

Plate 21

Most semi- (half) tones are in either category 1 or 2, a black note to a white or a white note to a black. Note that there are only TWO white note to white note semi-(half) tones . . . E to F and B to C.

Obviously two semi-(half) tones = one whole tone.
Therefore:

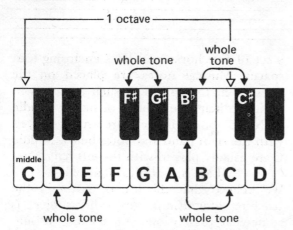

Plate 22

The distance between one whole tone and the next whole tone is twice the distance between a whole tone and the next semi-(half) tone.

There is always one key (white or black) between consecutive whole tones.

You remember in Lesson 1 that black notes occur in groups of two and three all the way up the keyboard. These black notes all get their names from the white notes on either side of them. You might like to think of a married lady who works. When she's at home she is called Mrs. Sharp. When she's at the office she is called Miss Flat. She is the same person in every way but she has two names depending on where she is at the moment . . her position at home, or her position at the office. In the same way you may call the black notes either Sharps or Flats provided you stick to one simple "positional" rule. This rule is concerned with whether you're going up the keyboard to the right, higher in terms of pitch, or whether you're going down the keyboard to the left, lower in terms of pitch.

Sharps
It might fix the word SHARP in your mind if you thought of the cost of living going up sharply. SHARP = UP. That is UP the keyboard, rising higher in terms of pitch.

12

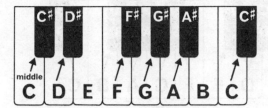

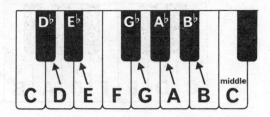

Plate 23

Plate 24

This is the sign for a SHARP: ♯

It raises the pitch of any note by one semi-(half) tone.

Watch the chart above while you play and say the named notes ten times each;

The black note immediately to the right of C going up (Sharp = Up) a semi-(half) tone in terms of pitch is C Sharp.

The next white note is D.

The black note immediately to the right of D going up a semi-(half) tone, rising in terms of pitch, is D Sharp.

The next white note is E.

The next white note is F.

The black note immediately to the right of F, going up a semi-(half) tone is F sharp.

The next white note is G.

The black note immediately to the right of G, going up a semi-(half) tone is G Sharp.

The next white note is A.

The note immediately to the right of A, going up a semi-(half) tone is A Sharp.

The next white note is B.

The next white note is C.

And the whole business starts all over again.

Have someone call out the Sharps—C Sharp, G Sharp, A Sharp, etc., and practise finding them instantly.

Flats

It might fix the word FLAT in your mind if you thought of falling down flat on your face. FLAT = DOWN. That is down the keyboard to the left, falling lower in terms of pitch.

This is the sign for a FLAT: ♭

It lowers the pitch of any note by one semi-(half) tone.

Watch the chart above while you play and say the named notes ten times each.

The white note immediately to the left of Middle C is B. The Black note immediately to the left of B, going (falling) down a semi-(half) tone, lower in terms of pitch, is B Flat.

The next white note is A.

The black note immediately to the left of A going down a semi-(half) tone, in terms of pitch, is A Flat.

The next white note is G.

The black note immediately to the left of G going down a semi-(half) tone is G Flat.

The next white note is F.

The next white note is E.

The black note immediately to the left of E going down a semi-(half) tone is E Flat.

The next white note is D.

The black note immediately to the left of D going down a semi-(half) tone is D Flat.

The next white note is C.

And the whole business starts all over again.

Now think back to our lady who is Mrs. Sharp at home but Miss Flat at the office.

In the same way each black note has two names.

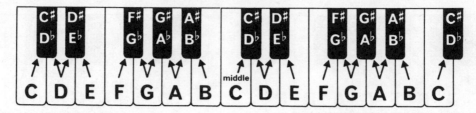

Plate 25

Watch the chart above as much as you can .. and at the same time say the following out loud and play the black notes involved—saying both their names as you play.

The black note going up a semi-(half) tone (SHARP) from white Middle C is C SHARP.

The same black note going down a semi-(half) tone (FLAT) from white D is D FLAT.

Think again of Mrs. Sharp at home but Miss Flat at the office. It is all a question of position, of where you are when you name the lady in question .. Mrs. Sharp or Miss Flat.

The black note going up a semi-(half) tone (SHARP) from white D is D SHARP.

The same black note going down a semi-(half) tone (FLAT) from white E is E FLAT.

The black note going up a semi-(half) tone (SHARP) from white F is F SHARP.

The same black note going down a semi-(half) tone (FLAT) from white G is G FLAT.

The black note going up a semi-(half) tone (SHARP) from white G is G SHARP.

The same black note going down a semi-(half) tone (FLAT) from white A is A FLAT.

The black note going up a semi-(half) tone (SHARP) from white A is A SHARP.

The same black note going down a semi-(half) tone (FLAT) from white B is B FLAT.

Practise saying and playing the black notes using both their names. Get thoroughly familiar with the following:

C SHARP IS D FLAT.   (C♯ IS D♭)
D SHARP IS E FLAT.   (D♯ IS E♭)
F SHARP IS G FLAT.   (F♯ IS G♭)
G SHARP IS A FLAT.   (G♯ IS A♭)
A SHARP IS B FLAT.   (A♯ IS B♭)

Note identification is a lot to take in, but it is the absolute foundation stone of your musical education. If you can't identify the notes quickly you are in the same position as trying to learn to read without being able to instantly recognise letters. You really only have to learn the names of seven white notes and the five black notes that are above and below them. And you must know all the notes equally well. It's either 100% or nothing. Think of how badly off you would be if you knew all the letters of the alphabet except "t".

Fif-y pence for a pin- of bi--er is -oo much. Fify doesn't make sense. Pin is a new word. Bier doesn't make sense in this context. Oo isn't a word and there you are! A pudding!

14

There are only twelve notes to learn, seven white and five black, so please practise. Have someone call out the notes to you mixing them up as follows:

D
D♭ (D FLAT)
G
C♯ (C SHARP)
A♭ (A FLAT)
B♭ (B FLAT)
F♯ (F SHARP)
G♭ (G FLAT)
Etc.

And try to find these notes as quickly as possible. It takes very very bright people about three hours of solid practice to learn to identify all the notes instantly. So don't get depressed if it takes you a little longer. Practise for a while and then have a pin- of bi--er .. or a cup of -ea.

An Octave
(From the Latin, Octo = 8, Octagon = an eight-sided figure), meaning eight consecutive notes. An octave can start on any note but must end on the same note either above or below, and both notes are counted to give eight. Think of an octave as a distance . . . and never mind what is in between for the moment.

So Middle C to the C above is an octave.

Middle C to the C below is an octave.

The C below Middle C to the C above Middle C is two octaves.

Any D to the next D above or below is an octave.

Any E to the next E above or below is an octave.

And so on.

A Scale
A Scale is the definite sequence of musical sounds going up or down. It can begin on any note but must end on the same note above or below.

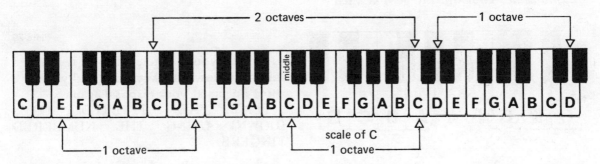

Plate 26

Using your first finger say and play the Scale of C from Middle C to the C two octaves above.

As you can see, using only one finger is a very inefficient way of playing the piano.

There are, however, some simple rules to follow when you use all five fingers. The rules are based on the following finger numbering.

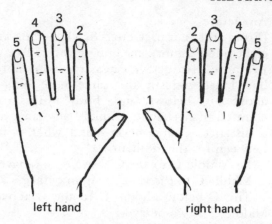

left hand   right hand

Plate 27

C.	D.	E.
1	2	3

SLIDE THUMB SMOOTHLY UNDER 3 TO

F.	G.	A.	B.	C.
1	2	3	4	5

Now reverse the whole process and come down the keyboard. Place your 5th finger on the C above Middle C. Play the first five notes down and again you have run out of fingers. So now you reverse the procedure. Instead of your "thumb under 3rd finger" play "3rd finger over thumb":

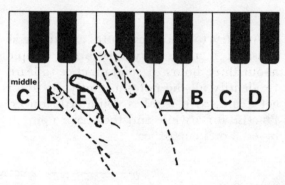

Plate 29

so that your whole hand is moved smoothly down the keyboard and you have three fingers at your disposal again.

PLAY THE LETTERED NOTES (DOWN) USING THE NUMBERED FINGERS.

C.	B.	A.	G.	F.
5	4	3	2	1

SLIDE THIRD FINGER SMOOTHLY OVER THUMB TO

E.	D.	C.
3	2	1

This is one octave of a C scale right hand. Practise it carefully. Each note should sound distinctly and be held down for the same amount of time.

Note that the thumb is number 1, your first finger is 2, etc.

We'll start with your right hand.

Place your thumb (1) on Middle C and play the first five notes. C. D. E. F. G.

By G you have run out of fingers. You can either lift you whole hand and start again with your thumb on A .. which is awkward and rough, or you can slide your *thumb under* your third finger like this:

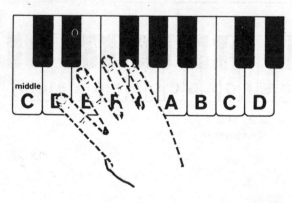

Plate 28

so that your whole hand is moved smoothly up the keyboard and you have five fingers at your disposal again.

PLAY THE LETTERED NOTES UP FROM MIDDLE C USING THE NUMBERED FINGERS.

Incidentally you'll be fascinated to learn that in the very early sixteen hundreds the thumb was considered a rather rude finger. It was considered terribly IN and very very good taste to play keyboard instruments WITHOUT using your thumb at all. Can you imagine going to a harpsichord recital in 1605, say, and being very annoyed because some awful, vulgar, low class player constantly used his thumb! It was an insane affectation and Bach spoke up against it calling it a load of rubbish. He more or less raised the thumb from its status of a poor relation to the one of leadership which it holds today.

Now let us learn the same scale down from Middle C with your left hand. Place your left thumb (1) on Middle C and play the first three notes down. Then smoothly slide your thumb under your third finger like this:

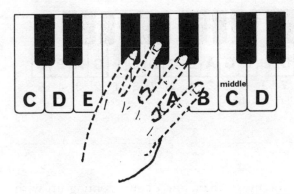

Plate 30

so that your whole hand is moved smoothly down the keyboard and you have five fingers at your disposal again.

PLAY THE LETTERED NOTES (DOWN) FROM MIDDLE C WITH THE LEFT HAND USING THE NUMBERED FINGERS.

C.	B.	A.
1	2	3

SLIDE THUMB SMOOTHLY UNDER 3 TO

G.	F.	E.	D.	C.
1	2	3	4	5

Now reverse the whole process and come UP the keyboard. Place your 5th finger on the C below Middle C. Play the first five notes UP and you have run out of fingers. So now you reverse the procedure. Instead of your "thumb under 3rd", play "3rd finger over thumb".

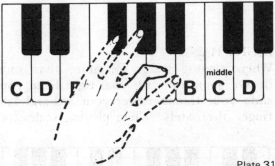

Plate 31

so that your whole hand is moved smoothly up the keyboard and you have three fingers at your disposal again.

PLAY THE LETTERED NOTES UP USING THE NUMBERED FINGERS.

C.	D.	E.	F.	G.
5	4	3	2	1

SLIDE THIRD FINGER SMOOTHLY OVER THUMB TO:

A.	B.	C.
3	2	1

You are now playing and correctly fingering one octave of the Scale of C up and down with your right hand and your left hand. Practise hands separately, playing the scale 50 times, smoothly and accurately. The notes should be even and of the same duration. The thumb under and third finger over movement should be smooth.

17

We would like now to enlarge your playing of the Scale of C to 2 octaves with each hand.

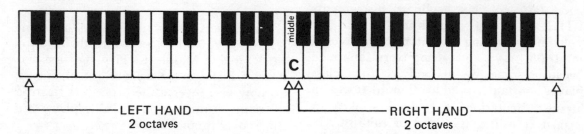

LEFT HAND
2 octaves   RIGHT HAND
2 octaves

Plate 32

RIGHT HAND

When playing scales for more than one octave going up with your right hand you slide your thumb under your 3rd and 4th finger alternately. When playing scales for more than one octave coming down with your right hand you put your 3rd finger and then your 4th finger alternately over your thumb.

C D E F G A B C D E F G A B C
1 2 3 1 2 3 4 1 2 3 1 2 3 4 5
RIGHT HAND

Plate 33

LEFT HAND

When playing scales for more than one octave going down with your left hand you slide your thumb under your 3rd and your 4th finger alternately. When playing scales for more than one octave coming up with your left hand you put your third finger and then your 4th finger alternately over your thumb.

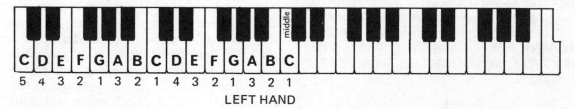

C D E F G A B C D E F G A B C
5 4 3 2 1 3 2 1 4 3 2 1 3 2 1
LEFT HAND

Plate 34

This is your first regular scale exercise. It is not terribly exciting but it's very important. Start all your practising by playing it 15 times with the right hand, then 15 times with the left, then 15 times together. Remember to try for smooth finger motion giving each note the same duration.

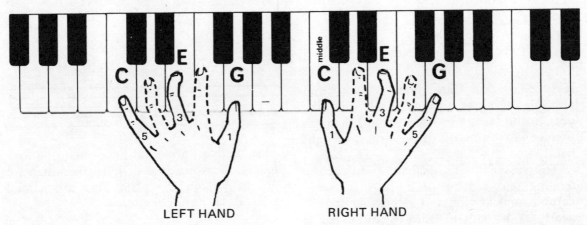

LEFT HAND   RIGHT HAND

Plate 35

Study this carefully. Note that your right hand thumb is on Middle C, 3rd on E, 5th on G.

Your left hand 5th is on the C below Middle C, 3rd on E, thumb on G.

This is called the C POSITION. It is the position in which both hands are ready to begin playing the C scale upwards. Accustom yourself to it. Practise finding it instantly.

With your left hand play C, E & G simultaneously. You are playing a simple triad (three) chord.

Any group of three or more notes played simultaneously is called a chord.

Now play JINGLE BELLS with both hands together . . . like this:

RIGHT HAND:	E. E. E.	E. E. E.	E. G. C. D. E.
LEFT HAND:	G	G	G	G
	E	E	E	E
	C	C	C	C

Congratulations! You've played a piece with both hands. And so endeth the second lesson . . . BLACK NOTES.

19

Lesson 3:
READING OF MUSIC RIGHT HAND

Now that you can quickly name and play all the notes on your piano we'd like you, in this lesson, to learn to read the ones you would ordinarily play with your right hand.

The system of musical notation—or the reading and writing of music—may seem complicated at first but remember it isn't nearly as difficult to learn to read music as to read the English language. The language has 26 letters with which you must be concerned, whereas music has only C. D. E. F. G. A. B.—seven. The object of this lesson is simply to get your fingers to obey—quickly and instinctively—an impulse that originates in the eye. The reaction might be compared to that of a good touch typist who can make her fingers touch particular keys without her ever taking her eyes off the page (music) she is copying (playing).

A few facts and definitions
You remember in Lesson 2 we talked about a "staff". This is the term used, generally, in North America. In England and Europe the word is STAVE. It can mean "diverting something unpleasant" in the sense that you stave off bankruptcy by borrowing more money or you can stave in your boat by banging into a rock. In music, however, a stave is our old friend:

a set of five horizontal lines enclosing four spaces. Now to go a little further than we did in Lesson 2 . . . the lines are named E. G. B. D. F. . . . like this:

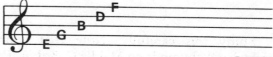

Plate 36

and the spaces are called F. A. C. E. . . . like this:

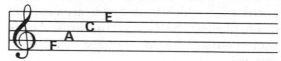

Plate 37

When we were kids we were taught that E. G. B. D. F. stood for Every Good Boy Does Fine, and that F. A. C. E. spelt simply "Face". Feel free if you want to be more adventurous—Evil Greek Bothered Defenceless Female or Fainting Actress Coughed Exhaustedly.

Draw yourself a stave on a spare sheet of paper.

Write in the lines, E. G. B. D. F.

Write in the spaces, F. A. C. E.

You have noticed that E. can be either the first line or the last space. This is because there are two E's on the stave. Remember, too, there is more than one E on your piano keyboard. There are, in fact, seven! In the same way F. can be either the first space or the last line. This is because there are two F's on the stave.

Now practise—by having somebody call out the following notes—which you will place in their proper position on the stave.

E. (1st line or 4th space)

C. (3rd space)

G. (Second line)

and   etc . . . F. G. C. E. D. B. E. D. A. C. G. F. C. E.

This rather strange sign—

Plate 38

which looks like a snake having a fit is called a TREBLE CLEF. Treble meaning "high" and clef from the Latin "clavis" for Key. Therefore "high key".

One of the earlier innovators in musical notation was an Italian named Guido d'Arezzo. Arezzo is a town in central Italy, hence Guido "of Arezzo". Guido dreamed up the stave but at first wrote the notes out in letters. These letters evolved into the clef signs of today, primarily two. This one:

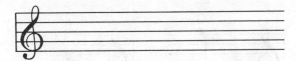

Plate 39

and another which you'll learn about later. The treble clef is also called the "G" clef and we think it might be a very fancy and old fashioned Italian "S", short for the Italian "Sol" or G. Anyway when you see this treble clef on a stave you know that all the notes are going to be above (higher in pitch) than Middle C.

Now since all the notes on this stave are above Middle C it seems only logical that Middle C should be BELOW the stave, like this:

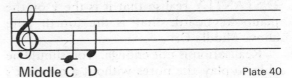

Middle C D   Plate 40

We obviously have an extra space immediately above and this is filled of course by the note above Middle C on the piano . . D.

This symbol ♩ . . . called a "note" means absolutely nothing by itself. But place it on a stave and it immediately becomes significant, a symbol of pitch. We are not, at the moment, dealing with time, rhythm or the *duration* of a note—we are discussing the note purely as a symbol of PITCH and not of TIME.

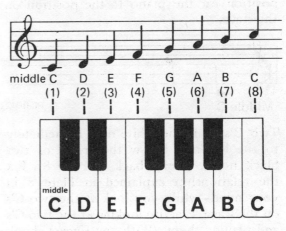

middle C D E F G A B C
(1) (2) (3) (4) (5) (6) (7) (8)

middle
C D E F G A B C

Plate 41

Study this stave carefully. You will notice that we have numbered the notes beginning with Middle C as 1, D as 2, E as 3, and so on. You should be able to look at the note E on the first line of the stave and INSTANTLY realise that it is the E on the piano keyboard, that is the third note above Middle C. You should be able to look at the note C on the third space of the stave and INSTANTLY realise that it is the C one octave (eight notes) above Middle C. You should be able to look at the note on the first space of the stave and INSTANTLY realise that it is the F on the piano keyboard, that is the fourth note above Middle C.

Realisation is not enough. You should be able to play the notes without a moment's hesitation. Again we go to the analogy of the touch typist. If she is really a touch typist . . she does not have to look at the letter C on a printed page and STOP TO THINK that she will play it (type it) with the third finger of her left hand "just below and to the left of F." She does this instantly.

In the same way your reactions must become instant and automatic. You will have to stop and think at the beginning—that is only natural, but try to relate visual position on the piano to the position on the stave.

Middle C

Plate 42

Two C's. C is the white note immediately to the left and below the group of two black notes. (Refer back to Plate 8). Fix the relationship explained in Plate 8 in your mind—while you look at the two C's on the stave. Practise looking at the two C's and playing them. (With any finger). Look and play. Over and over.

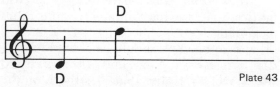

Plate 43

Remember that the white notes in the middle of each group of two black notes is always D. (Refer back to Plate 13). Fix the

relationship explained in Plate 13 clearly in your mind while you look at the two D's on the stave. Look and play. Over and over.

Plate 44

Remember that the white note immediately above (to the right of) each group of two black notes is always E. (Refer back to Plate 14). Fix the relationship explained in Plate 14 clearly in your mind while you look at the two E's on the stave above. Look and play. Over and over.

Plate 45

Remember that the white notes immediately below (to the left of) each group of three black notes is always F. (Refer back to Plate 15). Fix the relationship explained in Plate 15 clearly in your mind while you look at the two F's on the stave. Look and play. Over and over.

Repeat the above procedures for each of the following . .

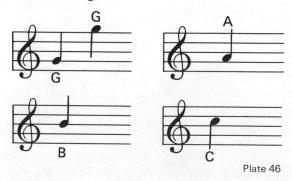

Plate 46

Practise these relationships, look and play.

Practise the following:
Keep your eye on the stave.
Play the indicated notes (with any finger you like).
Play them over and over until you can play the passage evenly and without hesitation.

Plate 47

(We have put in a bar | defined later, to help you keep your place.)

The relationship of written note (on page) to note (on keyboard) is exactly the same for all keyboard instruments, organ, harpsichord, piano and celeste. Incidentally we were trying to find out for you just when the very first organ was invented. We discovered that the instrument is mentioned several times in The Bible. In Genesis 21, Verse 4, we read .. "And his brother's name was Jubal, he was the father of all such as handle the organ." This got us delving into things Biblical and we discovered that David, of The Psalms fame, had a very large reputation as a musician and often sang his own Psalms and accompanied himself on an organ. David, as you may know is Hebrew for "beloved" or "loved one" and it's rather fascinating to imagine David around about 985 B.C. being a sort of pop idol. Possibly the leading Beatle of his day with the younger generation beating their breasts, tearing their hair out and generally going mad with pleasure over David's music.

While David may, indeed, have invented the organ there are some others in the running. Aristotle in 344 B.C. and Archimedes around 200 B.C. are both contenders. We tend to favour Archimedes for the simple reason that we rather like him as a lovable eccentric who leapt stark naked out of the bath and raced around with nothing on talking to whomever would listen about his famous Archimedes Principle. Anyway this got us off on a little Archimedian research and darned if we didn't come up with a picture. It's called The Archimedes Automatic Wind Instrumentalist and here he is:

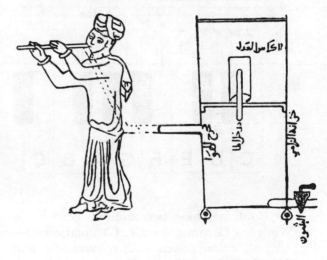

Plate 48

Can't you just imagine people asking this chap to a party and telling him to bring his Archimedes Automatic Wind Instrument!

Please go back and re-read the section on SHARPS in Lesson 2. This # is the sign for sharp. When it is placed in front of any note on the stave it raises the pitch of that note by a semi-(half) tone.

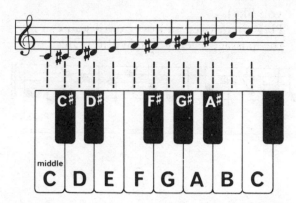

Plate 49

Now please go back and re-read the section on FLATS in Lesson 2. This ♭ is the sign for flat. When it is placed in front of any note on the stave it lowers the pitch of that note by a semi-(half) tone.

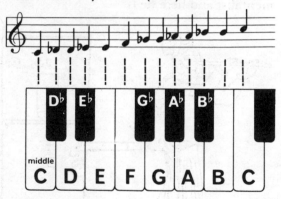

Plate 50

Combine these two and you get what is called a Chromatic scale. Chromatic meaning all colours, hence all colours of sound or pitch if you like. A Chromatic scale that begins on Middle C is written on the stave like this:

Now study the following carefully.

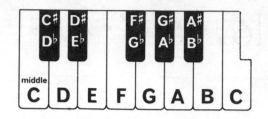

Plate 52

As we explained in Lesson 2:

C# is the same black note as D♭

D# is the same black note as E♭

F# is the same black note as G♭

G# is the same black note as A♭

A# is the same black note as B♭

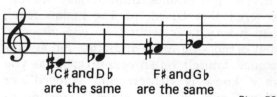

C# and D♭ are the same   F# and G♭ are the same

Plate 53

You remember we explained in Lesson 2 that there are two white note to white note semi-(half) tones: E to F and B to C.

Plate 51

24

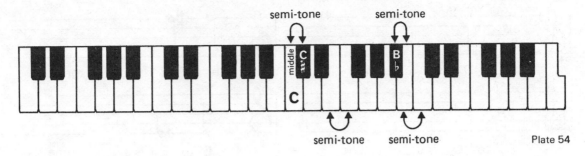

Plate 54

It becomes obvious that a whole tone is twice the distance of a semitone. Therefore there is always one key, either black or white, in between two consecutive whole tones.

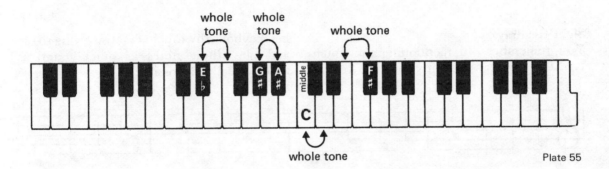

Plate 55

Exercises

In the following, state whether the distance between the notes is a whole tone or a semi- (half) tone.

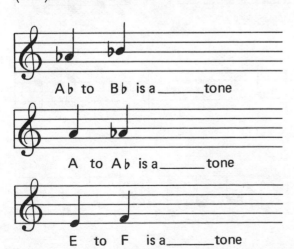

A♭ to B♭ is a _____ tone

A to A♭ is a _____ tone

E to F is a _____ tone

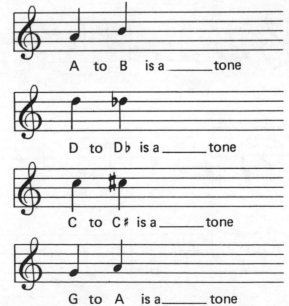

A to B is a _____ tone

D to D♭ is a _____ tone

C to C♯ is a _____ tone

G to A is a _____ tone

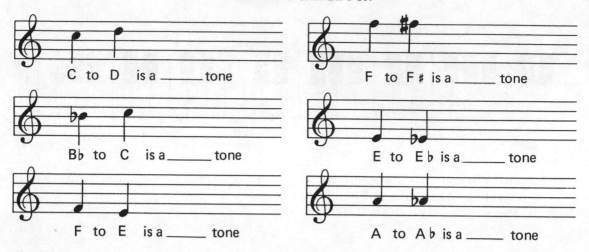

C to D is a _____ tone

F to F♯ is a _____ tone

B♭ to C is a _____ tone

E to E♭ is a _____ tone

F to E is a _____ tone

A to A♭ is a _____ tone

Plate 56

Sight Reading

You remember our mentioning the touch typist . . who can instantly locate a key on her keyboard by touch. Practise trying to say and play these notes as quickly and as automatically as possible.

Plate 57

Now practise having somebody call out notes quickly, and practise finding them instantly if not even faster:

B   E   C♯   B♭

A♭   C   F♯   D

G♯   C♯   B   G

G♭   D♭   D♭   F♯

F♯   G♭   E♭   A

D♯   G♯   G♯   A♯

Now we suggest you take a break for a cup of tea or a drink or a walk about the garden. We won't suggest this sort of thing

again since it's not our affair how you spend your time. But please don't try to take in *too much too fast*. This can be wearisome and confusing. If you're a super-brain that's different. But if you're the average intelligent individual remember that we've packed a large amount of information into this small volume and it is designed to be carefully *studied* not merely *read*. You *can* learn music and you *can* learn to play the piano. It isn't nearly as difficult as learning to read, write and speak the English language and you managed that successfully. But please take in Fact 1 and digest it thoroughly before you go on to Fact 2. If something confuses you read it out loud, figure it out on your piano keyboard before going any further.

To continue then.

Please go back to Lesson 2 and re-read the section on Scales and Fingering.

Here is the scale of C written on the stave. The numbers indicate the fingering.

1 2 3 1 2 3 4 5 4 3 2 1 3 2 1

Plate 58

Play it and watch the keys, saying the names of the notes.

Play it and watch the stave, saying the names of the notes.

Up until now you have been playing notes one after the other and one at a time. A Chord (from "Choral" meaning "singing together") is a group of three or more notes.

Study the following:

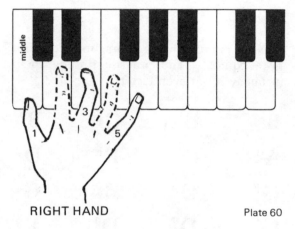

Plate 59

An INTERVAL is the distance (difference in pitch) between two notes, and is usually though not always measured from the tonic.

Thus you see that the interval (distance) between C and E is a THIRD. The interval between C and F is a FOURTH. The interval between C and G is a FIFTH. The interval between C and A is a SIXTH, the interval between C and B is a SEVENTH. The interval between Middle C and the C above is an eighth .. or OCTAVE.

Every chord is named from its "Tonic" (Tone) or Key Note. A TRIAD CHORD contains the Tonic or Key note, the 3rd

and the 5th. Thus:

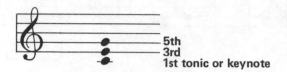

5th
3rd
1st tonic or keynote

represents the C Major Triad Chord, Tonic (C) Position, meaning that the tonic or Key Note (C) is at the bottom.

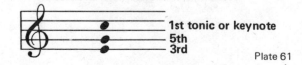

RIGHT HAND   Plate 60

Rest your fingers slightly curled, on the keyboard. Your hand is now in the C POSITION (which we discussed at the end of Lesson 2. Your 1st, 3rd and 5th fingers are on the 1st (note) C, 3rd (note) E, and 5th (note) G, of the Key of C. Play these three notes—the Major Triad of the Key of C. Take your hand off the piano, look away, then try to find and play the chord again accurately and quickly. Do this twenty-five times or until you can find the chord automatically.

You may play the notes of the chord in any position you wish. If, for example, you take the Tonic or Key Note and place it at the top of the chord, you get:

1st tonic or keynote
5th
3rd

Plate 61

Put your thumb on E, 3rd Finger on G, 5th Finger on C. Play it. This is still a C chord. Take you hand off the piano, look away, then try to find and play this chord automatically. This is called the First Inversion, the Tonic or Key Note is on the TOP (1st) of the chord.

If you place the Tonic or Key Note in the second position (from the top) you get:

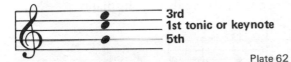

— 3rd
— 1st tonic or keynote
— 5th

Plate 62

Put your thumb on G, 3rd Finger on C and 5th Finger on E. This is still a chord. Take your hand off the piano and again practise finding this chord quickly and automatically. This is called the Second Inversion with the Tonic or Key Note in the second position from the top.

Note that chords are in the tonic or Key position when all the intervals (distances) of the Chord look alike—the distances between the notes being the same—so that all the notes in the chord are on lines or all on spaces.

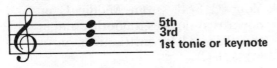

— 5th
— 3rd
— 1st tonic or keynote

G maj triad chord
tonic position
G is the tonic

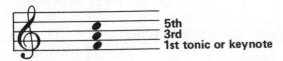

— 5th
— 3rd
— 1st tonic or keynote

F maj triad chord
tonic position
F is the tonic

Plate 63

Regardless of the position of the tonic, the three notes "sing together" and make a pleasant sound.

PITCH is that quality of a musical sound which depends on the rapidity of the vibrations producing it. When you play the A above Middle C the hammer hits the piano string and makes it vibrate 440 times in one second. This "rate of vibration" was decided upon in 1939 as British Standard Concert Pitch. The only really exact way pitch can be defined is in terms of vibrations per second.

A moment's thought will illustrate this. You cannot say that ♩ has any pitch because you do not know where it is on the stave. Once you place it on the stave you give it a set number of vibrations per second which you can compare (higher or lower) than A = 440. In the same way if you sing only a single note, you require a second note to say whether the first note is higher or lower. Pitch is the same phenomenon regardless of the instrument. In the case of an organ tuned to British Standard Concert Pitch a column of air vibrates at 440 cycles per second to produce the A above Middle C.

You can demonstrate the variables of Pitch yourself. Take two bottles the same size and shape, say two Coca Cola bottles. Fill one half, and the other three-quarters full of water. Blow into both bottles and you will hear a different pitch. You can alter the pitch by altering the level of the water in the bottle.

Sound is something very different from pitch. Sound might be described as the sensation produced in the ear when the surrounding air is set in vibration in such a way as to affect the organs of hearing. An explosion is a sound but not necessarily a Pitch. Under average conditions sound travels about twelve miles a minute, 720 miles an hour. This is slow enough to create certain problems under certain conditions. For instance, in a hall that is very long and narrow, where there are a large number of performers on a stage that is also rather deep and narrow, the sound from the most distant performer at the back of the stage reaches your ear perceptibly later than the sound from, say, the first violinist who is right at the very front of the stage. Another phenomenon that affects your enjoyment of music is the fact that sound travels faster through hot air than cold. So if a hall gets very hot towards the end of a concert the wind instruments tend to rise in pitch as the air inside them grows hotter and hotter and vibrates more rapidly. The rest of the orchestra, whose instruments are less susceptible to a higher temperature, try to follow, but this is impossible for the piano player who is stuck with the pitch of the piano as it is.

Take a long look at the following and then try playing it on your piano.

Plate 64

Play these notes evenly . . . and see if you recognise the melody. It is actually "LITTLE BROWN JUG" but it is written out without any indication of either rhythm or time—both subjects we will study in a future lesson.

Now that you know what the melody is, see if you can play it in the rhythm it was originally written in.

Here is "JINGLE BELLS" written out. You know the rhythm.

E 3 times   E 3 times   E G C D E

Plate 65

Practice is what separates the men from the boys. If you are adult in your approach and bring to your practising the right mental attitude you will enjoy it, make a bit of a game of it, and progress rapidly.

Practice for Lesson Three

1. Playing JINGLE BELLS in the proper rhythm with both hands.
2. Seeing notes on the Treble Clef Stave and automatically playing them on your piano.
3. Get any piece of music written in the Key of C (no sharps or flats) and practise playing single notes on the Treble Clef Stave. It will sound horrible but never mind.
4. Your C Scale from Middle C up and down two octaves, smoothly and evenly. (See Page 34 for instructions on practising scales.)
5. Playing LITTLE BROWN JUG in the proper rhythm keeping your eyes on the stave. Your eyes should not leap from keyboard to stave every time you play a note. "Feel" for the notes as much as you can. (Touch typing again.)
6. Your intervals. From C to E is a Third in the Key of C, F is a Fourth, etc.

If you practise one hour every day for two weeks you should know and understand this lesson thoroughly.

And so Endeth Lesson Three, THE READING OF MUSIC RIGHT HAND.

Lesson 4:
READING OF MUSIC LEFT HAND

By this time you should be able to read, name and automatically play all the notes on your piano above Middle C—which you would, ordinarily, play with your right hand. Someone once asked Serge Rachmaninov, the great Russian composer and pianist, what he considered the piano student's minimum requirements. Evidently in a sour mood, Rachmaninov replied: "A minimum of two hands with a minimum of five fingers on each." This does not mean, of course, that your basic equipment is the equal of his. You will feel "all thumbs" and clumsy at the moment but this awkwardness will gradually disappear with practice. Even though you may consider yourself musically untalented you can achieve reasonable proficiency and give yourself and your friends a great deal of pleasure.

Your position at the piano is important. Sit in such a way that the middle of you is opposite Middle C, keep your back fairly straight but relaxed. Keep your fingers slightly curved as though you were holding in your hand a fair-sized apple.

A few facts and definitions

f means "forte" from the Italian word for loud.

ff means "fortissimo" from the Italian for "very loud".

p means "piano" from the Italian for "softly".

pp means "pianissimo" from the Italian for "very softly".

There is some historical basis for retaining these words since the original composers used them and Italian was the language of the originators of music. We feel their use is slightly fatuous like the convention of printing French menus in an English restaurant. Most people like to know what they're eating, or listening to, or playing and we propose to use the English terms along with the Italian ones. This sign:

𝄢

which resembles a "C" written backwards is the Bass (pronounced "base") meaning low clef as opposed to the treble 𝄞 or "high" clef. When you see 𝄢 on a stave it means that all the notes written on the stave will be below Middle C and will ordinarily be played by the left hand. The word bass is applied to the deepest and lowest of men's voices and understandably to Basset hounds whose stomachs if they were any lower would be dragging on the ground.

When you see the Treble Clef on a stave you know that all the notes are going to be *above* Middle C and when you see the Bass Clef on a stave you know that all the notes are going to be *below* Middle C.

Middle C, then, is BETWEEN the two staves.

Plate 67

The LINES in the Bass Clef are G. B. D. F. A.

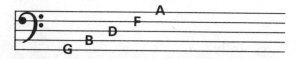

The SPACES in the Bass Clef are A. C. E. G.

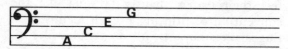

Plate 68

As kids we were taught that G. B. D. F. A. stood for "Good Boys Don't Fool Around" and A. C. E. G. stood for "All Cows Eat Grass." There are several extremely vulgar word combinations for both the lines and the spaces which we shall not mention on the theory that if your mind is that way inclined they will have occurred to you already and if your mind is not that way inclined, far be it from us to contribute to your moral depravity. Use any word combination you like but commit the letters of the lines and spaces to memory.

Draw yourself a stave on a spare sheet of paper. Put in the Bass Clef. Write in the lines .. G. B. D. F. A. Write in the spaces .. A. C. E. G.

As with the Treble Clef you will notice that some notes appear on the stave in two positions. G can be the fourth space or the first line. Similarly A can be the first space or the fifth line.

Practise learning these lines and spaces exactly the way you learned the ones in the Treble Clef. Have somebody call out the following notes—which you will place in their proper position on the stave:

G   B

A   E

F   G

G   F

C   C

E   E

D

and etc. Practise until you can write the notes on the stave without a moment's hesitation. It should be as automatic as your ability to instantly write T. H. E. if we say "the".

In exactly the same way that you learned the notes on the Treble Clef, try to relate visual position on the piano to the position on the stave. Let us start with the first line of the Bass Clef—G. Lines are G. B. D. F. A. and spaces are A. C. E. G.

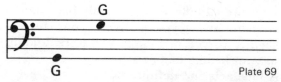

Plate 69

The white note immediately above (to the right of) the first black note in each group of three is always G. Refer back to Plate 16. Practise looking at these two G's and playing them. Look and play. Over and over. There are two G's on the Bass Clef Stave.

A

A

Plate 70

The white note immediately above (to the right of) the second black note in each group of three is always A. Refer back to Plate 17. Practise looking at these two A's and playing them. Look and play. Over and over. There are two A's on the Bass Clef Stave.

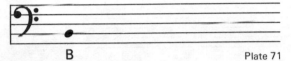

B

Plate 71

The white note immediately above (to the right of) the third black note in each group of three is always B. Refer back to Plate 18. Look at this B and play it. Look and play. Over and over.

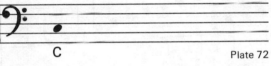

C

Plate 72

This is second space C. It is eight notes away from Middle C .. down, i.e. lower in pitch. Look at this C and play it. Look and play. Over and over.

Repeat the above procedure for each of the following and refer back to the plate indicated.

(Plate 13)   (Plate 14)   (Plate 15)

D   E   F

Plate 73

Here is a simple passage for you to play with your left hand. Try to keep your eyes on the stave and "feel" for the notes if you can. If you can't "feel" then feel free to look—but it's the "touch typist approach" that we want. Try to use the fingers we've indicated (numbered). Play the passage over and over again (fifty times is not too often) until you can play the whole thing without once looking at your keyboard. Practise playing *f* forte, (loudly), and *p* piano (softly).

5 3 2 1   1 2 3 4   5 4 2 1   1 2 3 5

5 5 2 2   1 1 5 5   5 4 3 2   1 2 3 4

5 2 1 2   4 2 3 4   5 3 1 2   1 2 4 3

Plate 74

(We have put in a bar | defined later, to help you keep your place.)

Middle C is the first line below the Treble Clef and the first line above the Bass Clef as

you have seen. Some notes, then, can be either below the Treble Clef or above the Bass Clef and be in the same position. Observe the following:

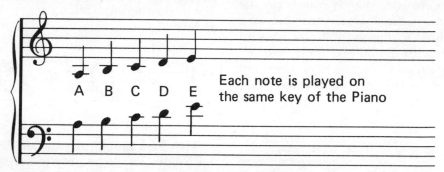

Each note is played on the same key of the Piano

Plate 75

Each pair of notes (above) is identical and is played on the same key of the piano.

Lines or spaces which occur above or below the staves are called Leger Lines and

Leger Spaces.

Please go back and thoroughly review right and left hand fingering (Plates 33 and 34) in Lesson 2.

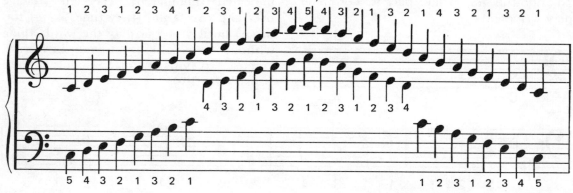

Plate 76

Remember we are still not concerned with time signatures or the duration of the notes as this comes in Lesson 5. What we are concerned with is that you play these scales (and all the others you'll be learning) in a certain way. Please adhere to the following rules for all scale practising and remember the thumbs go under and fingers come over evenly and smoothly.

Scale Practice

1. Play the right hand alone, slowly and smoothly twenty times.

2. Play the left hand alone, slowly and smoothly twenty times.
3. Play both hands together very loudly twenty times.
4. Play both hands together very softly twenty times.

We are now going to learn special names for two other important "C's" on the keyboard. 2nd space C on the Bass Clef is the C one octave (eight notes) below Middle C. 3rd space C on the Treble Clef is the C one octave above Middle C.

So consider the following:

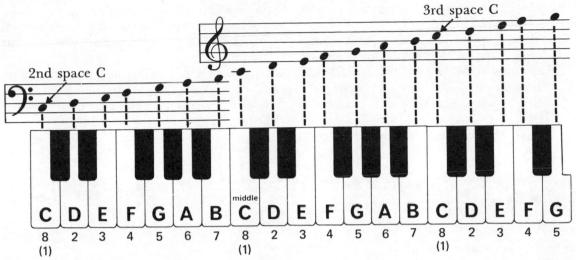

Plate 77

Notice that our numbering is consistent. In the Key of C, C is always 1, D is always 2, E is always 3, F is always 4, G is always 5, A is always 6 and B is always 7.

Consider the Bass Clef stave for a moment. You should be able to look at the third space E and instantly realise it is the third note above 2nd space C. You should be able to look at the fourth space G and instantly realise it is the 5th note above second space C.

Again we bring up the case of our touch typist of whom you must be thoroughly sick by now. Mentally practise relating notes to their nearest C. The fifth line A in the Bass Clef stave is closer to Middle C than to second space C. Think of it as three notes down from Middle C and at the same time as six notes up from second space C. Remember that C is always 1. The second line G in the Treble Clef stave is five notes above Middle C or four notes below third space C.

In Lesson 3 you learned that an interval is the distance (difference in pitch) between two notes. The rules governing intervals apply to both clefs, Treble and Bass, in exactly the same way. These may seem very complicated but we promise you they aren't. Read the previous three paragraphs aloud, pausing to consult the chart, count slowly, and you will see that the relationships are very simple mathematically. The process involved in learning musical notation is not nearly as difficult as that experienced by a small child in learning to read English. Put your left hand second finger on Middle C. With your right hand play E . . . and say out loud . . "E is the third (note) above Middle C." You count C as 1, D as 2, E as 3. It isn't complicated at all really. Then play the A above your (still held down) Middle C. Count C as 1, D as 2, E as 3, F as 4, G as 5 and A as 6. Then say out loud . . "A is the sixth (note) above Middle C." Do this for all the notes in the C Scale from Middle C up to "third space C".

Now put your left hand second finger on second space C and with your right hand play the E above it. Again you see that "E is the third (note) above C" . . and the relationship holds good no matter what C on the piano you choose to count from.

Ponder, say out loud, and play the following intervals:

35

Middle C down to the E below is a sixth. (Count it . . !)

Middle C up to the F above is a fourth.

Middle C down to the A below is a third.

The A above Middle C down to Middle C is a sixth.

Third space C up to the F above is a fourth.

The G below Middle C down to second space C is a fifth.

Second space C up to the G above is a fifth. (exactly the same distance or interval)

In Lesson 3 you learned the Chromatic (all colours = all notes) for the right hand. Here it is written on the Bass Clef stave for the left hand.

Plate 78

Here is the Chromatic Scale starting on C, one octave, for both hands.

Plate 79

Note that if you play Middle C with the right hand and move "up" the keyboard, playing all the black and white notes one after the other in order until you reach the white B below third space C—you have moved up a distance of twelve notes or steps. Count them. Each step is the same distance (interval) and consists of a semi-(half) tone. This, then, is the Chromatic Scale built on C. You can start on any note you like. After you have taken the twelve equi-distant steps you are back on your original note again but an octave higher. This takes a moment's thought so don't skip. Begin on various notes and count out your twelve steps and you'll see that you're always back on the note you started from.

We apologise for being repetitious but it's terribly important that you grasp these relationships thoroughly.

36

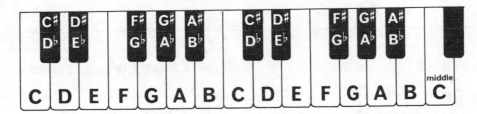

Plate 80

Study this along with Plate 52 shown here again.

C sharp is the same black note as D flat.
D sharp is the same black note as E flat.
F sharp is the same black note as G flat.

G sharp is the same black note as A flat.
A sharp is the same black note as B flat.
Translate this onto the Bass Clef stave and we get:

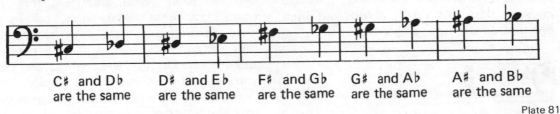

C♯ and D♭ are the same   D♯ and E♭ are the same   F♯ and G♭ are the same   G♯ and A♭ are the same   A♯ and B♭ are the same

Plate 81

And exactly as in the Treble Clef there are two white-note-to-white-note semi-(half) tones. E to F and B to C.

Review the little test you did in Lesson 3, Plate 56. Now do the same test except that the notes are written on the Bass Clef Stave.

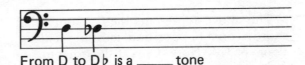

From D to D♭ is a _____ tone

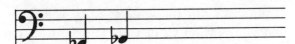

From A♭ to B♭ is a whole tone

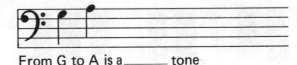

From G to A is a_____ tone

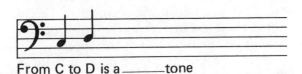

From C to D is a_____tone

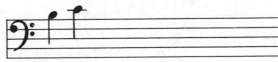

From B to C is a _____ tone

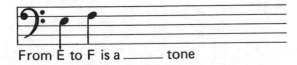

From E to F is a _____ tone

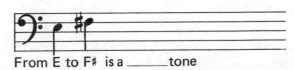

From E to F♯ is a_____tone

37

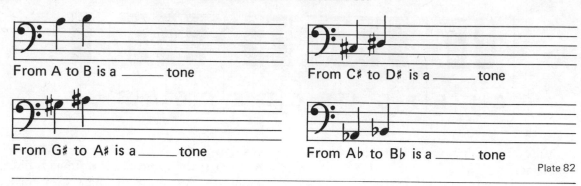

From A to B is a _____ tone

From C♯ to D♯ is a_____ tone

From G♯ to A♯ is a_____ tone

From A♭ to B♭ is a _____ tone

Plate 82

Bass Clef Chords

The intervals involved are exactly the same in both Bass and Treble chords but their position on the stave is different.

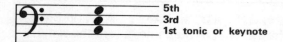

5th
3rd
1st tonic or keynote

Plate 83

The above represents the C Major Triad chord, Tonic (C) position, meaning that the Tonic or Key Note (C) is at the bottom.

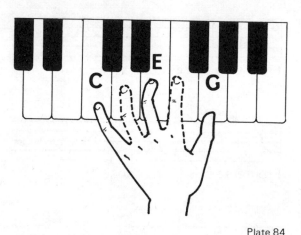

Plate 84

This the C POSITION (LEFT HAND). Compare this with Plate 60 which shows

you exactly the same thing for the Treble Clef and Right Hand. Practise in the same way. Play these three notes, take your hand off the piano, look away, then try to find and play the chord again accurately and quickly. Do this twenty-five times until you can find the chord automatically.

Again, as with the Treble Clef you may play the notes of the chord in any position you wish. If you take the Tonic or Key Note and place it at the TOP of the chord, you get:

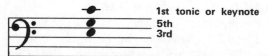

1st tonic or keynote
5th
3rd

Plate 85

Put your 5th finger on E, your 3rd on G and your 1st on C. Play it. This is still a C chord. Take your hand off the piano, look away, then try to find and play this chord accurately and quickly. Do this until you can find the chord automatically. This is called the First Inversion, the Tonic or Key Note is on the top (1st) of the chord.

If you place the Tonic or Key Note in the second position from the top you get:

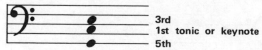

3rd
1st tonic or keynote
5th

Plate 86

38

Put your 5th finger on G, your 3rd on C and your 1st on E. This is still a C chord. Take your hand off the piano and again practise finding this chord quickly and automatically. This is called the Second Inversion with the Tonic or Key Note in the second position from the top.

As in the Treble Clef the chords are in the Tonic or Key position when all the intervals (distances) of the chord look alike—the distances between the notes being the same—so that all the notes in the chord are on lines or all on spaces.

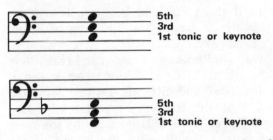

Plate 87

As in the Treble Clef, any combination of the Tonic, 1st and 3rd "sing together" and make a pleasant sound.

KEY SIGNATURE means, literally, the "Sign of the Key." Dwell on the word a moment. Think of a Key as something that unlocks or opens up the way to something. There is also the connotation that a Key explains something that is unknown—the "key to the mystery." So a Key Signature is an "indicator" if you like, something that points the way for you. You also think of a key on the piano as being any one of the white or black notes. You know by now that the "Key Note" of the scale of C is C.

The Key Signature is written at the beginning of each line of music immediately after the Treble and Bass Clefs. It is made up of one or more sharps or one or more flats but never a mixture of both.

When there is no Key Signature the piece is in the Key of C Major.

Memorise the following simple rule even though you don't understand it for the moment:

THE ORDER OF SHARP KEYS GOES UP IN FIFTHS AND THE ORDER OF FLAT KEYS GOES DOWN IN FIFTHS.

Look at Middle C on your piano. The 5th above (going up) is the note G. Therefore the Number 1 Sharp Key is called G Major.

The Key Signature looks like this:

Plate 88

The minute you see this Key Signature you should instantly deduce the following:

There is one sharp in the Key Signature, F♯.

The number 1 Sharp Key is called G Major.

Therefore the piece is written in the Key of G Major.

All the "F's" regardless of their position on the piano keyboard or the staves are played as F♯.

In the Key of G Major all the notes in the piece relate to each other in the same way as the notes in the Scale of G Major.

These deductions should bring you, without too much pain, to this concept of the Scale of G Major.

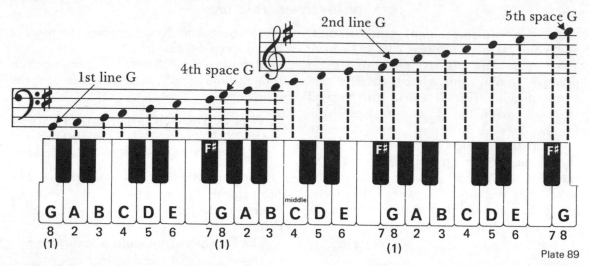

1st line G 4th space G 2nd line G 5th space G

F# F# F#

G A B C D E | G A B C D E | G A B C D E | G
8 2 3 4 5 6 | 7 8 2 3 4 5 6 | 7 8 2 3 4 5 6 | 7 8
(1)   (1)   (1)

middle

Plate 89

Now try to shut the Key of C completely out of your mind for a moment. THINK in the Key of G. It is not quite like thinking in a different language because the names of the notes are the same in both keys. But you must think five tones higher. Hear five tones higher.

Refer back to Plate 77 for a moment.

Now look at Plate 89.

In the Key of G, G is always 1, A is always 2, B is always 3, C is always 4, D is always 5, E is always 6, F♯ is always 7.

The mathematical relationships are identical with the Key of C. 1 is always the Key Note, in this case G. In the Key of G you are *counting from G*, remember.

Therefore if we ask you to play a C Major 3rd you would play C (1) and E (3).

If we ask you to play a G Major 3rd you would play G (1) and B (3).

Practise finding and counting your intervals in the Key of G Major. B is the 3rd as we've said. C is the 4th. D is the 5th. E is the 6th. F♯ is the 7th.

All the positional and visual relationships remain constant. The white note immediately below (to the left of) each group of three black notes is still F. All the mathematical relationships are the same. The C above G is a 4th. Count it. Count out all the other intervals. Identical. Once you've learned them for one key you've learned them for all keys. Get the hang of it and it's dead easy.

We won't suggest a tea break here although we'd like to since this lesson is complicated and difficult. Instead, we'll tell you that the reason the piano keyboard isn't longer from bottom note to top note has nothing to do with the length of the human arm but a great deal to do with the human ear. The highest note on your piano represents a frequency of about 4,000, meaning that the top note string vibrates back and forth four thousand times in one second. The lowest note on your piano represents a frequency of about 35 and this is approaching the lower limits of pitch where it begins to turn into "noise". Acoustics, or the science of sound, is an enormously complicated subject and as far as the piano is concerned there are many variables involved such as the length, diameter and tension of the strings as well as the materials of which they are made, i.e. copper, steel.

You'll enjoy your piano much more if it is tuned regularly. Twice a year is minimal and once every quarter is preferable.

You are now "thinking" in the Key of G Major.

40

So:

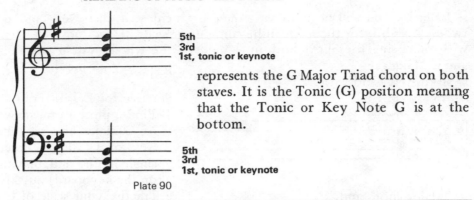

5th
3rd
1st, tonic or keynote

5th
3rd
1st, tonic or keynote

Plate 90

represents the G Major Triad chord on both staves. It is the Tonic (G) position meaning that the Tonic or Key Note G is at the bottom.

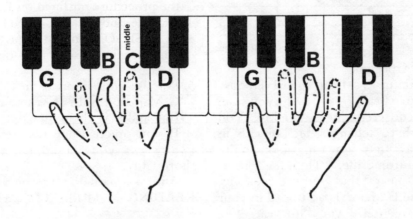

Plate 91

This is the G POSITION. Compare it to the C POSITION in Plate 60. Practise it in exactly the same way. Play the notes, take your hands off the piano, look away, then try to find and play the chords with both hands accurately and quickly. Do this twenty-five times until you can find the G POSITION with both hands automatically.

ARPEGGIO comes from the Italian word "arpa" meaning harp and means to play the notes of a chord one after the other rather than simultaneously. Arpeggios occur in several forms but for the moment we will be concerned only with those which start on the Tonic or Key

Note. *Think* in C Major and—
Note that:

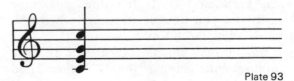

Plate 93

is a C Major chord and that:

Plate 92

is a C Major Arpeggio.

41

Later on you will begin playing them in two octaves but for the moment be content with practising the above both in C Major and G Major.

In the left hand we get:

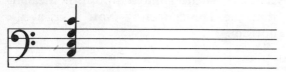

Plate 94

a C Major chord and:

Plate 95

is a C Major Arpeggio.

Now think in G Major again! Practise "tuning your brain" so that you can "think" in different keys quickly. You should be able to "change gears" quickly in the same way that you can when you're driving an automobile. "Thinking" in C Major really means that you are mentally "hearing" the C Major Triad Chord in your mind. Then mentally you "up gear" five notes and you are thinking in G Major meaning that you are mentally "hearing" the G Major Triad Chord in your mind. You'll get the hang of it if you look away from the piano and sing C. E. and G. Then sing G. B. and D. If this does not come easily to you now it will later when you know a few more Key Signatures.

So "think" in G Major and practise finding and playing the G Major Triad Chord in its Tonic and First and Second Inversions. You'll find all the Scales in all the Key Signatures, together with their Arpeggios, written out in full at the back of this book.

Please remember what we said about your attitude to practising at the end of Lesson 3. Make a game of it and you'll enjoy it. Persevere and don't be discouraged. Before too long a light will go on and the whole system will fall beautifully into place in your mind.

Practice for Lesson Four

1. Find a piece of music written in the Key of C Major and another written in the Key of G Major. Practise picking out single notes and playing (finding them on the keyboard) quickly.
2. Practise your scale of C Major following the procedure outlined on Page 34.
3. Practise your Scale of G Major following the procedure outlined on Page 34.
4. Practise finding the C POSITION and the G POSITION on both staves with both hands quickly—so that it becomes automatic.
5. Practise your intervals in C Major and in G Major on both staves so that you can find and play them quickly.

If you practise one hour every day for two weeks you should know this lesson thoroughly.

And so endeth Lesson Four, THE READING OF MUSIC LEFT HAND.

Lesson 5:
TIME AND NOTES

A Conductor is a man who stands up in front of an orchestra and waves his arms around. To be a good one requires a very high degree of musicianship. He is called a "Conductor" or a "leader" because he is supposed to be conducting the orchestra (or leading it) from the beginning of the piece to the end. You can appreciate that if you have fifty or more highly individualistic musicians with their varied hang-ups and idiosyncrasies *somebody* has to see that they all get to the same place at the same time. It is almost like keeping fifty soldiers (with *their* varied hang-ups) marching in step together. If one soldier gets seriously out of step the whole platoon looks ragged and sloppy. What is more the disease spreads until half a dozen are out of step and before long you have a mob scene rather than a group of marching men. In music you can think of time as the duration of one note compared to the duration of another.

A few facts and definitions
CONCERTO is a composition for a solo instrument accompanied by an orchestra.

SYMPHONY literally means a "concord of sound" and is specifically applied to an elaborate composition for a large orchestra in three or more movements (sections).

A BAR LINE is a vertical line drawn across the staves to mark the metrical

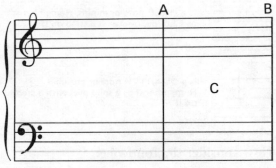

Plate 96

(measurable and regular) accent.

A and B are Bar Lines. The space between them, C, is called simply a bar. Bar also means the transverse ridge of a horse's palate, a bank of sand, or a place you go to get drunk in. But a bar in music is a place we put notes into and we can put in almost as many notes as we wish provided the notes have certain relationships to each other. People drive themselves mad trying to sort out these relationships and we have never been able to understand why. So we propose to start the explanation with some very elementary mathematics.

The following relationships are very simple arithmetically and you have no problems in understanding them:

$$1 = 2 \times 1/2$$
$$1 = 4 \times 1/4$$
$$1 = 8 \times 1/8$$
$$1 = 16 \times 1/16$$
$$1 = 32 \times 1/32$$

Note that all these lines mean exactly the same thing and therefore each line is equal to *every other line*. This is abundantly self-evident when we're dealing in simple arithmetic but it is slightly more complicated when we're dealing with symbols (notes) rather than numbers.

So don't dismiss the arithmetic as too elementary.

It is obvious that:

32/32nds = 16/16ths = 8/8ths = 4/4ths = 2/halves = 1.

It is this simple arithmetical relationship on which all the note relationships in music are built.

 is a WHOLE note or semibreve. Remember it as a hollow oval or a polo mint if you like

 is a HALF note or minim. Remember it as a hollow oval with a stem on it

is a QUARTER note or crotchet. Remember it as a solid oval with a stem on it

 is an EIGHTH note or quaver. Remember it as a solid oval with a stem on it and *one* little flag at the top of the stem

 is a SIXTEENTH note or semiquaver. Remember it as a solid oval with a stem on it and *two* little flags at the top of the stem. (It will quaver twice as fast.)

 is a THIRTY SECOND note or demi-semiquaver. Remember it as a solid oval with a stem on it and *three* little flags at the top of the stem. (It will quaver four times as fast as a one flag quaver.) Plate 97

Now consider the following:

= 1 whole note or semibreve

= 2 half notes or minims

= 4 Quarter notes or crotchets

=8 Eighth notes or quavers

=16 Sixteenth notes or semiquavers

= 32 Thirty-second notes or demisemiquavers

Plate 98

44

When 8th notes or quavers, 16th notes or semiquavers and 32nd notes or demi-semiquavers appear in groups they are joined together with bars for ease of writing. 1 Bar = 1 little flag; 2 bars = 2 little flags and 3 bars = 3 little flags.

Each line in Plate 98 is equal to every other line in terms of duration. Every line is equal to every other line in terms of arithmetic as we explained on Page 43.

Ponder this with the greatest care because it is the essence of musical time. Europe uses the terms minims, crotchets, quavers, semiquavers and demisemiquavers, but North America uses the easier grasped whole, half, quarter, eighth, sixteenth and thirty-second. If you expect to pass any musical examinations in Europe or play with European musicians you're stuck with the longer and clumsier names. On the other hand, if you see yourself strictly as a "solo" artist then use the easier whole, half, quarter terminology.

TIME SIGNATURE means, literally, "the sign of the time". The Time Signature consists, always, of two numbers written one above the other and it is written immediately after the Key Signature on both staves at the beginning of a piece of music.

Remember that the arithmetical relationships explained in Plate 98 are *constant* no matter what the Time Signature may be.

When you see:

Plate 99

you know at once that the piece is written in the Key Signature of G Major and that the Time Signature is ¼. The top number always means the number of counts or beats to the bar. The bottom number indicates what type (duration) of note gets one count, in this case a quarter note or crotchet. So immediately you say to yourself . . "Four beats in each bar and a quarter note (crotchet) gets one beat".

Similarly:

Plate 100

means there are three beats in each bar and a quarter note (crotchet) gets one beat.

2/4 means there are two beats in each bar and a quarter note (crotchet) gets one beat.

6/8 means there are six beats in each bar and an eighth note (quaver) gets one beat.

4/4 is by far the most "common" Time Signature and it is frequently indicated by a large "C", as in Plate 101.

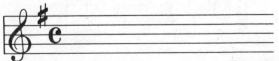

Plate 101

45

Play the following and count out loud:

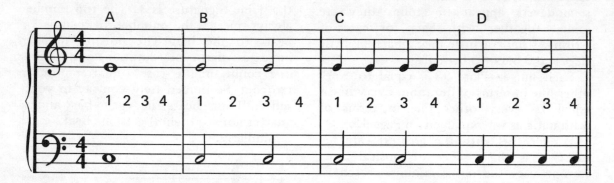

Plate 102

Your Time Signature ⁴₄ tells you at a glance that there are 4 beats to each bar and that a quarter note (crotchet) gets one beat.

So in Bar A
You count 4 beats to one whole note (semibreve)

In Bar B
You count 2 beats each to 2 half notes (minims)

In Bar C
In the Right Hand you count 1 beat to each of the 4 quarter notes (crotchets). Left Hand 2 beats to each of the 2 half notes (minims).

In Bar D
In the Right Hand you count 2 beats to each of the two half notes (minims). Left Hand 1 beat to each of the 4 quarter notes (crotchets).

Now try this one:

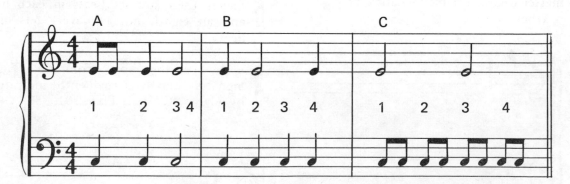

Plate 103

So in Bar A
Right Hand: 1 beat to 2 eighth notes (quavers), 1 beat to the 1 quarter note (crotchet) and 2 beats to the 1 half note (minim). Total 4.

Left Hand: 1 beat each to the 2 quarter notes (crotchets), 2 beats to the 1 half note (minim). Total 4.

In Bar B
Right Hand: 1 beat to the first quarter note (crotchet), 2 beats to the next half note (minim) and 1 beat to the last quarter note (crotchet). Total 4.

Left Hand: 1 beat each to the 4 quarter notes (crotchets). Total 4.

In Bar C
Right Hand: 2 beats each to the two half notes (minims). Total 4.

Left Hand: 1 beat to each group of two eighth notes (quavers). Total 4.

See if you can play the following:

Arr. Junkin—Ornadel

Plate 104

If it did not sound reasonably like JINGLE BELLS then you are doing something wrong. Count evenly and slowly and try it again.

You have now played (and what is more important READ) your piece from Lesson 1.

Now be a sport and try the whole piece. Take it very slowly and count evenly and smoothly.

Plate 105

48

*in the 8th bar. The ♮ is known as the "natural sign". It means that the preceding sharp or flat should be dispensed with and the note played as F natural—meaning it is neither sharpened or flattened.

JINGLE BELLS is entirely made up of whole notes (semibreves), quarter notes (crotchets) and half notes (minims).

When you see the sign > above a note it means it is to be "accented" or played with greater emphasis. Consider the difference between the pronounciation of the following:

FABulous
FaBUlous
FabuLOUS

You correctly say FABulous by accenting the first syllable of the word and this is exactly what > an accent means in music.

Now be a little bit more adventurous and try the following. Play it with the right hand only .. but count it carefully. Accent beats 1 and 3 slightly and you'll get a bit more "swing" to it.

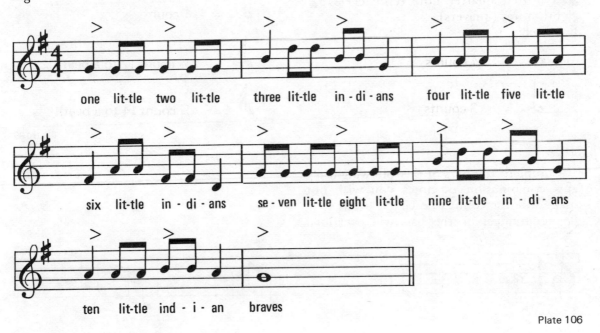

Plate 106

Now try to make complete bars of the following so that each bar counts out correctly using only quarter notes (crotchets)

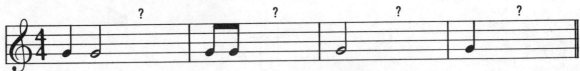

Plate 107

Now make complete bars of the following using only eighth notes (quavers)

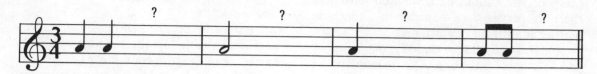

Plate 108

A dot **.** placed after a note increases its time value by ½. So:

♩**.** a dotted half note (minim) = 3 ♩ quarter notes (crochets).

♩**.** a dotted quarter note (crochet) = 3 ♪ eighth notes (quavers).

In ¼ time:

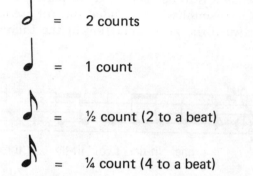

𝅗𝅥	=	2 counts	
♩	=	1 count	
𝗈	=	4 counts	♪ = ½ count (2 to a beat)
♩**.**	=	3 counts	♬ = ¼ count (4 to a beat)

Plate 109

Complete the bars of the following using any combination of notes you wish but make sure the count to each bar totals 4.
Be economical or the bars will overflow.

Plate 110

50

Complete the bars of the following but
make sure the count to each bar totals 3.

Plate 111

Complete the bars of the following but
make sure the count to each bar totals 2.

Plate 112

⅜ time means 6 beats to a bar and an eighth note (quaver) gets one beat. Complete the bars of the following, using any combination of notes you wish, but make sure the count to each bar totals 6.

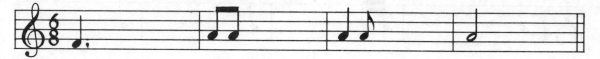

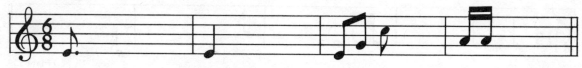

Plate 113

After ¼ time, ¾ time is the next most common time signature. Think of Common ¼ time being cut in half to ¾.

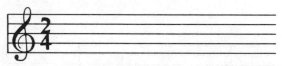

Plate 114

Just a few more ingredients to very nearly complete your knowledge of Time as far as notes are concerned. A Tie in music is written like this ⌢. It means that two notes are "tied together". The first note is held for the time value of both notes together. Ties may occur within a bar and from one bar to the next. You frequently see this at the end of a piece:

Plate 115

Remember, too, that dotted notes are like tied notes, thus:

Plate 116

A vertical wavy line like this ∫ preceding a chord means that the notes of the chord are to be played separately. "Rolled" if you like, with a rolling motion of the hand and wrist.

Plate 117

Ritardando, usually written *Rit*. means to play gradually slower. Accelerando, usually written *Accel*. means to play gradually faster.

All this business of time and note values may seem frightfully complicated to you at the moment but it becomes obvious and simple if you analyse it carefully. We haven't come to "rests" (silences) yet but we will in the next chapter. For the moment, however, just concern yourself with note values. Take any piece of music you like and ignore all bars which contain rests. Try to make the "note-only" bars count out correctly in accordance with the Time Signature. Think about notes as you would arithmetic. The following doesn't confuse you one bit:

$$1 + 1 + 1 + 1 = 4$$
$$1 + 1 + (1/2 + 1/2) + (1/4 + 1/4 + 1/4 + 1/4) = 4$$
$$1/2 + 1/2 + 1/4 + 1/4 + 1/4 + 1/4 + 1/4 + 1/4 + 1/4 + 1/4 + 1 = 4$$
$$1 + 1/8 + 1/8 + 1/8 + 1/8 + 1/8 + 1/8 + 1/8 + 1/8 + 1 + 1 = 4$$

The reason it's so easy is that you look at 1/2 and INSTANTLY know there are 2 of them in 1. Or you look at 1/4 and INSTANTLY know there are 4 of them in 1. When you can look at ♪ and instantly know there are two of them in ♩ or look at ♩ and instantly know there are two of them in ♩ your problems are solved. You'll find the whole pattern will suddenly click into place and become as simple as the arithmetical relationships explained above.

So keep at it!

And this brings us to a piece of equipment called a Metronome, meaning literally "Time Regulator". There are several varieties on the market and it would be wise to invest in one. Buy an inexpensive one and keep it away from the kids. They

all work the same way (metronomes not kids) on the principle of an inverted pendulum with a sliding weight which can be moved up and down so that when the pendulum swings the machine emits a regular series of "clicks" at whatever speed you select with the sliding weight. They look like this:

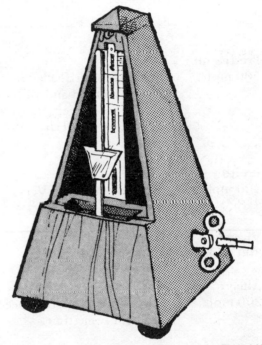

Plate 118

Use it to practise with so that you give every note its exact value and each bar the same duration in time. Use it particularly when you're practising your scales so that you develop an even regular touch. Mind you, music is only rarely played in absolutely strict time. Marches are sometimes exceptions and so are dances but even some dances get faster and faster towards the end so that they work up to a big climax.

But the point is that you can't speed up a piece or slow it down or generally take liberties with it until you can play it in strict time giving every note its exact value. Look at Time as your boss. Don't take liberties with him until you know him very well.

Here are some words you may encounter at the beginning of a piece of music. All of them relate to Tempo—that is the "time" or rate of speed at which the piece is to be played. They're in Italian simply because so much of music originated in Italy. They're pretentious today but there you are. Why call a girl an "ecdysiast" when you mean she's a stripper. The terms are arranged in descending order of speed, the fastest at the top. Since they're all relative we've put in miles per hour to give you something of the comparisons involved.

Prestissimo:
500 mph
Space ship stuff! Play it as fast as you can and still hit all the notes. Very dangerous except for the technically skilled.

Presto:
400 mph
Fire brigade stuff. Very, very fast.

Vivace:
300 mph
Ambulance. Very fast.

Allegro:
200 mph
Fast. Your suggested speed limit for some time.

Animato:
100 mph
Fairly fast, slower than Allegro.

Allegretto:
75 mph
A good clip but slower than Animato.

Moderato:
60 mph
Means what it says. A nice moderate speed.

Andante:
45 mph
Moderately slow and distinct.

Lento:
30 mph
Slowly and somewhat stately.

Adagio:
15 mph
Very slowly and very stately.

Largo:
10 mph
Very, very slowly, a bride up the aisle.

Grave:
5 mph
Funeral march stuff. Any slower and you'd come to a stop.

Now let us see what you can do with this old nursery rhyme which you may recognise as "BAA BAA BLACKSHEEP". Set your metronome mark at Andante 66. Practise it by playing the right hand alone 10 times, giving each note its correct value. Then play the left hand alone ten times. Then try putting them together. Remember ¼ time means four beats to the bar and a quarter note (crotchet) gets one beat.

Plate 119

Here is the same piece written in ⁴⁄₄ time, using 8th notes (quavers) instead of quarter notes (crotchets).

Plate 120

Here is another old traditional air. Practise it in exactly the same way. First the right hand ten times, then the left ten times, then put them together.

Moderato

Arr. Junkin/Ornadel

Plate 121

A note here about sight reading music.

When you are reading a newspaper and come across the word "push", you instantly take in the four letters as a *group*. You do *not* go through the whole alphabet to relate P with the U with the S with the H. You instantly see the whole word not the individual letters.

In the same way, when you are reading music and you come across:

Plate 122

Try not to read the notes *separately* as C. D. E. F.

Instead you should instantly see that the first note is Middle C and that you are required to play a line, then a space, then a line, then a space, starting at Middle C. You know these notes follow each other on the piano with *nothing in between*. So "bingo"! You see these four notes as a *group* or a *word* if you like.

In the same way when you see:

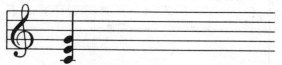

Plate 123

you should instantly realise that you are seeing three "line" notes in a chord. There is a space (a note) in between each one.

You do *not* think C. E. G. You see the three notes as a *group*—the 1st, 3rd and 5th of the C Major Scale. (Refer back to Plate 60)

Try to develop these "concepts" in the Key of C and the Key of G Major. You'll find that the same combinations occur frequently in the same way that the words "and" and "is" and "but" occur frequently in the English language. So read *groups of notes* (words) rather than single notes (letters). Go through pieces of music in the Key of C or G Major and look for groups of notes that occur frequently.

Practice

1. Repeat Practice Note 2 from Lesson 4. Now use your Metronome and strive for smoothness and evenness.
2. Repeat Practice Note 3 from Lesson 1 in the same way.
3. Repeat Practice Note 5 from Lesson 4.
4. Practise BAA BAA BLACKSHEEP and the TRADITIONAL AIR in this lesson until you can play both of them smoothly and without hesitation. We'll come to interpretation later but if you want to "ham up" the TRADITIONAL AIR go ahead. Think of it as "very sad" and play it that way. Think of it as "calm and serene and lovely" and play it that way.
5. Thoroughly memorise your note values. Take any piece of music and look for bars that contain no rests. (Rests are dealt with in the next lesson). See if you can make the bars count out correctly according to the time signature. If you practise one hour every day for two weeks on this lesson you should know it thoroughly.

And so endeth Lesson 5, TIME AND NOTES.

Lesson 6:
RHYTHM AND RESTS

Rhythm is many things. It is measured recurrence; it is pulse; it is the regulated succession of strong and weak elements; it is flow. You encounter rhythm in almost anything that moves. Swimming, dancing, the movement of the waves breaking on a beach. Musically, rhythm can be defined as the movement of notes with respect to time; that is how fast notes move (tempo) and the patterns of long and short notes as well as of accents. Listen to any piece of music and it quickly becomes obvious that some notes stand out more than others. They may stand out because they are louder than the notes around them, dynamic accent; they may stand out because they are higher or lower than the notes around them (tonic accent); or they may stand out because they are held for a longer time (agogic accent). In some music the first beat of a bar tends to stand out as in the *1-2-3, 1-2-3,* of a waltz. You will frequently find in ¾ time that the first beat is accented and that the third beat is accented slightly less.

Here is TWINKLE-TWINKLE LITTLE STAR in two versions. Ponder the difference between:

Plate 124

where the "accent" seems to fall naturally on the first and third beat and:

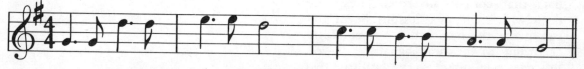

Plate 125

where the rhythm is altered by lengthening the first note in each bar by one-half of a beat.

This alteration does not make too much difference in this simple tune—but you see how "rhythm" is as much a part of what the music is saying as the notes.

Rhythm affects the meaning and feel of a piece of music in much the same way as it affects the meaning and feel of speech. Consider the following sentences:

1. CAN you play golf with me today?
2. Can YOU play golf with me today?
3. Can you play GOLF with me today?
4. Can you play golf with ME today?
5. Can you play golf with me TODAY?

Each sentence contains exactly the same English words in exactly the same order. But altering the emphasis or accent (rhythm) gives each sentence a diffcrent meaning. Sentence 1 suggests dubious availability of the person being spoken to. Sentence 2 suggests that the person being spoken to represents a desperate last choice as a golfing partner. 3 suggests that the person being spoken to has been asked to play other games but has refused. 4 suggests that the person being spoken to has refused to play golf with other people and 5 suggests that there has been some disagreement about the day of the week.

These differences in meaning are important and might seem very subtle indeed to a person who is not thoroughly at home in the English language. The accented word gives each sentence its own peculiar colour and implication. In the same way rhythm gives meaning and colour to music and its combinations are almost limitlessly variable. An accent may occur on short notes as well as long, soft notes as well as loud, lower notes as well as higher ones and where it is placed seems to be determined by a large number of variables whose interaction is not precisely known. So finally we must say that rhythm is understandable as an experience but undefinable in terms of cause.

Rhythm is very often what you want to make it. You hear the clickety-clackety repetitive rhythm of a speeding train. Depending on your mood this might sug-gest escape and hope or the inevitability of approaching doom. You hear the slower, smoother rhythm of waves breaking on a beach. Again depending on your mood this might suggest safety and solidity or it might suggest being steadily beaten down into a pulverised heap.

Frequently sheer loudness or softness gives a completely different meaning (colour) to one word (or note). "Help" said in a whisper, as the last gasp of a dying man, means something very different to "Help!!!!" shrieked at the top of your voice and calculated to bring swift assistance from the fire brigade or police.

Remember, too, that rhythm exists in any repetitive sound as well as in music. You can clap your hands or tap your desk in such a way as to produce rhythm without producing music.

By this time you have realised that rhythm has no accurate definition. So in order to develop a personal sense of rhythm of your own you must be able to play a piece of music exactly as it is written in terms of time.

You think of the word "rest" as a period of relief from regular activity; a period of doing nothing. It means exactly the same thing in music. Before we get to the actual rests in music consider what a pause adds to a simple sentence.

1. Can you loan me (PAUSE) a pound?
2. Can you (PAUSE) loan me a pound?

1 suggests that you are uncertain as to whether to ask for one pound or two.

2 suggests that you are uncertain as to whether the person being spoken to will loan you money under any circumstances regardless of the amount.

A few facts and definitions
ABSOLUTE PITCH: the ability to identify a musical note by name or to sing a particular tone without the help of first hearing some other tone. Also known as

"perfect" pitch, it actually consists of the ability to remember sounds. Try it. Have somebody play a note on your piano and see if you can name it correctly without looking at the keyboard.

ANTHEM: a short choral piece with a text based on the Bible or some other religious source and performed during the service in various churches.

ARIA: from the Italian for "air" or "song". An elaborate solo song, generally with instrumental accompaniment, usually used in connection with an opera. Arias are also important in cantatas and oratorios.

CANTATA: A composition for voices and instrumental accompaniment consisting of several movements. It is like an oratorio but is generally shorter and not necessarily confined to a religious subject.

ORATORIO: Similar to a Cantata but usually based on a religious theme. An oratorio is performed without scenery, costumes or action. The story is told through the music. The word comes from oratory, a chapel in a church.

REST: A period of silence which is written in different shapes depending on how long it is to last.

Here are the note values with their equivalent rests.

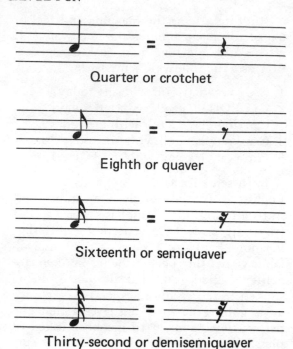

Quarter or crotchet

Eighth or quaver

Sixteenth or semiquaver

Thirty-second or demisemiquaver

Plate 126

Study these rests carefully. As you did with notes try to get so that you recognise them instantly.

It is now obvious that a bar of music can be made up of:

All notes.

Some notes + some rests.

All rests.

Therefore you see how the arithmetical relationships explained on page 53 can deal with either notes or rests or a combination of both. Obviously you can't have a piece that is *all* rests unless you can hear a piano *not* being played. Hopefully you are now thoroughly at home with Plate 98. Exactly the same arithmetical relationships hold good for rests.

Note   Rest

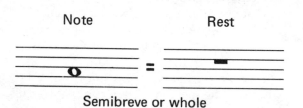

Semibreve or whole

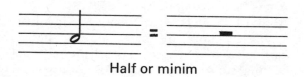

Half or minim

$$1 \; \rule{0.5em}{0.4em} \; = 2 \; \rule{0.5em}{0.4em} \; = 4 \; \text{ᗺ} \; = 8 \; \text{૪} \; = 16 \; \text{૪} \; = 32 \; \text{૪}$$

Plate 127

Review the simple arithmetic involved in note values and apply them to rest values.

There are various rules for the correct writing of music which we will ignore for the moment and concentrate on the arithmetic involved. It is dead easy. Suppose you are asked to complete the following bar, using either notes or rests or a combination of both in anyway you like.

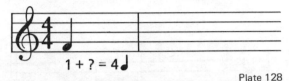

Plate 128

You know from the Time Signature that there are 4 beats to each bar and that each quarter note (crotchet) gets 1 beat. Therefore you know that each bar must "add up" to the equivalent of 4 quarter notes (crotchets). Here is one choice:

Plate 129

Here is another:

Plate 130

Here is yet another:

Plate 131

Now you can take any piece of music you like and make the bars count out correctly in accordance with the Time Signature. Begin with the exercises below.

Complete the bars of the following using any combination of rests and notes you wish but make sure the count to each bar totals 4 quarter notes (crotchets).

Plate 132

Complete the bars of the following using any combination of rests and notes you wish but make sure the count to each bar totals 3 ♩ quarter notes (crotchets).

Plate 133

Complete the bars of the following using any combination of rests and notes you wish but make sure the count to each bar totals 6 ♪ eighth notes (quavers). Again, be economical or the bars will overflow.

Plate 134

Please practise doing this—and practise taking any piece of music you like and counting out each bar in accordance with the Time Signature. Do this for half your practice time for two weeks. It seems confusing and difficult at first, but once you've become used to it the whole pattern will click into place. It seems difficult because you're dealing with ♩ and ♪ instead of numbers.

You'll remember from Lesson 4 that:
THE ORDER OF SHARP KEYS GOES UP IN FIFTHS AND THE ORDER OF FLAT KEYS GOES DOWN IN FIFTHS.

Look at Middle C on your piano. The 5th note below (going down) is F. Therefore the No. 1 Flat Key is called F Major.

The key signature looks like this:

Plate 135

The minute you see this Key Signature you should instantly deduce the following:

There is one flat in the Key Signature, B♭.

The No. 1 Flat Key is called F Major.

The piece is written in the Key of F Major.

All the B's, regardless of their position on the piano or on the staves are played as B♭.

The Key of F Major means that all the notes in the piece will relate to each other in the same way as the notes in the Scale of F Major.

The distance between the notes (intervals) are exactly the same as for the Keys of C and G Major.

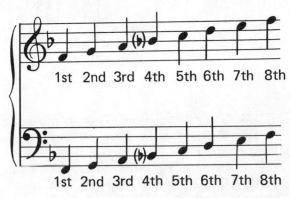

1st 2nd 3rd 4th 5th 6th 7th 8th

1st 2nd 3rd 4th 5th 6th 7th 8th

Plate 136

Therefore if we ask you to play an F Major third you will play an F and an A. In the Key of F Major F is always 1, G 2, etc. Practise finding and counting your intervals in the Key of F Major. Again try "thinking" in the Key of F Major. So:

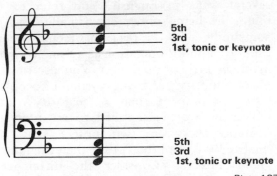

5th
3rd
1st, tonic or keynote

5th
3rd
1st, tonic or keynote

Plate 137

Plate 137 represents the F Major Triad Chord on both staves. It is the Tonic (F) position meaning that the tonic or Key Note F is at the bottom.

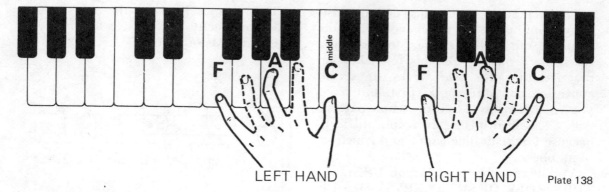

LEFT HAND   RIGHT HAND   Plate 138

This is the F position. Again compare it to the C Position in Plate 60 and the G Position in Plate 91. Practise it in exactly the same way. Play the notes, take your hands off the piano, look away, then try to find and play the chords with both hands accurately and quickly. Do this twenty-five times until you can find the F Position with both hands automatically. Practise "singing" the notes F. A. C. to yourself so that you are "thinking" in the Key of F Major. Add the F Major Scale and arpeggio (written out at the back of the book) to your practice schedule.

We now come to something called "Minor". The word literally means "small" or "smaller than". You use the word in several ways in English. You refer to a minor as being under age (smaller than) somebody who is over eighteen. You think of a minor operation as a "small" one involving little or no danger. You also think of a "minority" as being a group of people lesser in number than a "majority". In music the word is applied to an interval (distance between two notes) that is smaller by a semi-(half) tone than the same Major Interval. Consider the difference between:

and

Plate 139

You observe that the distance between C and E Flat is smaller than the interval between C and E Natural. You will also notice that the Minor chord sounds "sadder" or more mournful if you like, than the Major chord.

A moment's thought shows you that if we ask you to play a C Major Third you would play C and E Natural. A C Minor Third and you would play C and E Flat.

There are three forms of the minor scale but we shall be concerned with only one. The Harmonic.

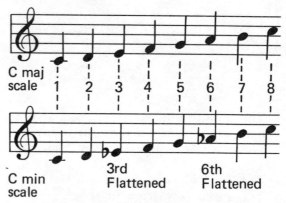

C maj scale   1   2   3   4   5   6   7   8

C min scale   3rd Flattened   6th Flattened

Plate 140

You observe that the Harmonic Minor of any Major scale is formed by lowering (flatting) the third and sixth interval by a semi-(half) tone. The fingering is the same as that used in the Major Scale.

The Scales of F Major and G Major (indeed all Major Scales) are converted to their Harmonic Minors in exactly the same way. Study these scales as written out in the back of the book. Practise them with their arpeggios.

Composers choose Minor Keys to write about sad things, grief, unrequited love, death, etc., because the flatted 3rd and 6th gives the Key a "sad" quality. Compare the difference between the first two bars of "Swannee River" written in the Key of C Major:

Plate 141

with the same thing written in C Minor.

Plate 142

*Note that the E Flat at the beginning of this bar holds for all the E's which occur within the bar. The same rule holds for sharps.

All we have done in the above is to flat the third (E) and the sixth (A) and the song takes on an entirely different mood.

Your basic knowledge of note values is now complete except for Triplets.

A TRIPLET as the word implies means three. It is a group of three notes of the same time value played in the time usually taken for two notes.

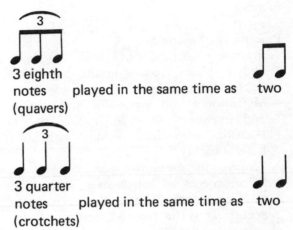

3 eighth notes (quavers) played in the same time as two

3 quarter notes (crotchets) played in the same time as two

Plate 143

Observe the difference between:

Eighth notes or quavers

Count: 1 2 3 4 1 2 3 4

and the same thing in triplets.

Count: 1 2 3 4 1 2 3 4

Plate 144

Triplets are always marked by the slur line and a number 3.

Both these passages take exactly the same amount of time to play. The Metronome count is the same in both. In the first passage you are playing two eighth notes (quavers) to a beat and in the second one you are playing three eighth notes (quavers) to a beat. The notes under the slur line, that is within the triplet, should be played in a smooth and connected manner.

Practice for Lesson Six

1. Practise your Scales of C Major, D Major and F Major, following the procedure outlined on Page 34. Now use your Metronome and strive for smoothness and evenness. Practise finding the F Position on both staves and with both hands quickly.
2. Thoroughly memorise your rest values.
3. Select pieces of music in ¾, ¾, ¼ and ⅜ time and count the bars out correctly according to the Time Signature.
4. Practise your scales in C Minor, D Minor and F Minor, following the procedure outlined on Page 34. From now on use your Metronome with all your scale practising.
5. Now begin to practise your scales in what is called "contrary" (opposite) motion. This means that your right hand is going up while your left hand is going down. Notice that your "thumbs under" and "fingers over" occur at the same spot, the same fingers being used simultaneously in both hands.

Below is one octave of the Scale of C Major in Contrary Motion.

You are now in possession of all the basic elements involved in the reading of piano music. Get so familiar with them that they become a part of you. If you practise one hour every day for two weeks on this lesson you should know it thoroughly.

And so endeth Lesson Six, RESTS AND RHYTHM.

Plate 145

Lesson 7:
PEDALLING AND PHRASING

By now, if you have been thorough in your practising and taken one step at a time, you should have a good basic knowledge of how music is written, how to read it, and how to relate what is written on the staves to the piano keyboard. Please don't move on to the Chopin Prelude we give you in this lesson unless you can instantly recognise rest and note values. Continue to devote as much time as you can to going through music in ¾, ⅜, ¼ and ⅝ time making each bar count out correctly in accordance with the Time Signature. You do not need to be near a piano to do this, you can do it anywhere. You might consider it a profitable way of spending the time it takes you to travel to and from your work.

You are about to move into areas which many students do not attempt until their second or third year of piano lessons. We are moving much more rapidly because, as we said in the preface, we are not attempting to develop your talent to the point where you can give a recital in the Festival Hall. Your object in studying this book is to become a competent amateur not a professional concert pianist. This is a thoroughly worth while ambition in any field of art so don't be put off by the fact that you are never going to be a world famous pianist. It is odd, and we think mistaken, that people feel no sense of embarrassment at being classified as amateur cricketers or bridge players but tend to denigrate amateurism in music, acting or painting.

A few facts and definitions

MOVEMENT. A major section in a long orchestral or instrumental work such as a sonata, symphony or concerto. Usually such a section can stand alone but is related in some way to the rest of the work. It nearly always has its own Key Signature and tempo indication. Frequently, but not always, there is a brief pause between successive movements of a composition.

ETUDE. From the French, "study". An instrumental piece designed to improve the player's technique but which may contain very beautiful music. The finest examples are the piano études of Chopin about which more later.

PRELUDE. Literally "to play before", something that prepares the way for something or serves as an introduction. Today the word refers to short independent piano compositions in one movement. Chopin wrote twenty-four of them, all gorgeous and some fiendishly difficult. Other famous examples are twenty or so by Rachmaninoff. Great emotional binges if you ever become proficient enough technically. Have a go anyway.

WALTZ. A dance, as you know, always in ¾ time and always with the accent on the first beat. Some gorgeous ones by Johann Strauss. Chopin, Liszt, Beethoven, Schubert all wrote waltzes mainly for piano.

MINUET. Another dance form, in moderate tempo and ¾ time. It originated as a country dance and became fashionable in the court of Louis XIV.

BALLADE. The name for a dramatic instrumental piece sometimes, but not always, influenced by a traditional poem of some sort. Chopin wrote four of them, all gorgeous and difficult. They were inspired by some poems of a Polish poet, Adam Mickiewicz.

SERENADE. A love song sung during the evening below the window of a girl's bedroom. The singer usually has only one thought in mind and the serenade is supposed to get the message across.

BARCAROLLE. A type of song sung by the gondoliers of Venice or a musical composition imitating this type of song. Usually in 6/8 or 12/8 time, the Barcarolle has a regular accompaniment that suggests the steady rocking of a gondola. There are many barcarolles for the piano by Chopin, Mendelssohn and others.

RHAPSODY. A title used for a relatively short composition, free in form, usually expressing a particular mood. Frequently rhapsodies are based on a "national idea" such as Liszt's "Hungarian Rhapsodies". Sometimes a rhapsody is based on a folk tune or even on music by another composer, such as Rachmaninoff's "Rhapsody on a Theme of Paganini".

IMPROMPTU. The name given to a short keyboard piece that sounds as if it might have been improvised.

Incidentally we are giving you all these definitions so that when we come to interpretation you can "think about" the music.

TARANTELLA. A fast dance in 6/8 time in which the music keeps moving from a Major Key to a Minor Key and back again. The dance gets faster and faster ending in a very rapid tempo and a big climax. Chopin and Liszt wrote short, very fast pieces in this style.

CRESCENDO. A direction to play gradually louder and the operative word is *gradually*. It is either written "cresc." or indicated by the sign:

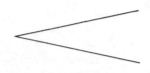

Plate 146

DIMINUENDO. A direction to play *gradually* softer. It is either written "dim." or indicated by the sign:

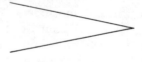

Plate 147

LEGATO. A direction to play as smoothly as oil without a break in between the notes.

STACCATO. A direction to play a note and get off it fast! Play the note quickly, lightly, and separately from the notes before and after it. Staccato is indicated by a dot over or under the note to be so played, as in Plate 148.

Plate 148

A little digression here about practising and concentrating. When you "concentrate" on something you try to exclude all other things from your mind and bring the object into the sharpest possible focus. It is very difficult to do well for a long period of time. Suppose we give you an apple and tell you to concentrate on it for five minutes. In a matter of *seconds* your mind will begin to wander because you lack motivation. But if we tell you to speculate as to why the apple is greener on one side than on the other, why it has a stem, what it is made of, how it grew, etc., you are able without too much effort to think continuously about it. So in order to concentrate on music you must think not only about it but around it.

If you are practising a section of a piece of music and you play it over and over be sure you give yourself a reason for each repetition. This applies to anything you are practising. The reasons for repetition in order of importance are:

1. Notation. To make sure you are playing the correct notes.
2. Tempo. To make sure you are giving each note the correct value.
3. Expression. To make sure you are giving the piece the colour you want in terms of loudness and softness, phrasing and pedalling.

Scale practice can easily become boring unless you approach it with interested concentration. The aim behind it is to teach technical facility, smoothness of touch and mental control of the fingers. So practise your scales (and anything else) in as many different ways as you can. Work in as much *contrast* as you can. Practise scales very loudly, then very softly. Are the loud notes as even and smooth as the soft ones? Practise scales accenting every other note, then every third note, then every fourth note. Above all listen to yourself. Is the scale smooth? Can you achieve a gradual crescendo and a gradual diminuendo so that the note at the top of the scale has exactly the same volume as the note at the bottom of the scale?

As far as pieces are concerned ask yourself what you are trying to achieve musically. If you are playing a love song can you make it more *loving*? If you are playing a march can you make it more inspirational? Etc. We'll develop this more in the lesson dealing with interpretation but apply this sort of musical thinking as much as you can from now on.

PEDALLING. You will recall from Lesson One that the right foot pedal on a piano is called the sustaining or damper pedal. Refer to Plates 1 and 2. Every book you pick up (including this one) will say that the damper pedal is incorrectly called the "loud" pedal. This is faintly pretentious like saying it is wrong to call a pound a "quid" or a dollar a "buck". Calling the damper pedal the "loud" pedal neatly distinguishes it from the left foot pedal which is called the "soft" pedal. We will bow to the purists but you can call the damper pedal anything you like so long as you learn how to use it.

The dampers on the piano are the strips of felt that are in contact with the strings at all times. There are one, two or three strings for each note according to the pitch. The single strings at the treble end are so short they don't need dampers.

When a key is depressed the damper belonging to that key automatically lifts in order to allow its string (or strings) to vibrate. This sustains the tone until the vibration of the strings gradually stops through inertia. When you release the key the damper automatically lowers against the strings, stopping their vibration, and silencing their sound. Try playing a C Major Triad Chord beginning on Middle C and holding it. You hear that the notes sustain.

Now depress the damper pedal and hold it down while you play the same chord again. You will hear the sound is richer and fuller because the whole instrument is "more alive" with sympathetic vibrations.

Now depress second space C (the C one octave below Middle C, remember?) so gently and slowly that you make no sound. Hold second space C down with your left hand and play Middle C sharply and quickly with your other hand lifting it instantly. You will hear the strings of second space C vibrating in sympathy even though they have not been touched with the key hammer.

With the damper pedal down play a C Major Triad Chord and lift your hand. Immediately play a hard quick D Flat octave. The tonal effect is unpleasant. The harmonies "fight" each other.

With the damper pedal down and starting on Middle C play C. E. G. and third space C one after the other. The effect is bell-like and pleasant because all the notes are related and together form a chord.

You should deduce from these little experiments that if the pedal is being used in a passage it must be changed for each change in harmony.

Pedalling is marked in music in a variety of ways.

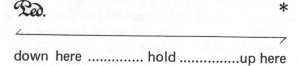

down here .... hold ....up here

Plate 149

The use of the pedal is to add "colour" as well as to sustain the notes after your fingers have left the keys. It can make or break your playing so think about it carefully.

Try the following exercise. Begin counting 1. 2. 1. 2. regularly. Then at 1 play an octave and hold it down. At 2 depress the damper pedal and hold it. You may now move your hand because the depressed pedal will hold (sustain) the sound. At the

next 1 play the next octave and at the same moment that you play raise your foot. (As the keys go down you raise your foot). Hold the octave until you count 2 then put the pedal down again. Continue the exercise slowly until you can depress the pedal exactly between the octaves and raise the foot the moment you play the next. It is written thus:

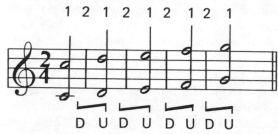

Plate 150

You can tell whether your pedalling is right or wrong depending on the sound. If you hear a complete "nice" chain of clear sounds without breaks in the smoothness you are doing the exercise correctly.

To control the pedal keep the ball of your foot on it and press it rather than stamp on it. Your heel should not leave the floor.

As you develop your pedal sense you'll learn to use it sparingly. Sometimes you should rely totally on finger legato.

So the pedal is used to give colour and richness to chords, especially in slow music, but in pieces that move along at a good clip be discreet. The damper pedal is like gin. A little is pleasing. Too much is sickening.

Here are some general rules.

1. Play first then pedal.
2. Change pedal for every change of harmony. Change pedal at the moment of playing.
3. Use with discretion to give colour to music.
4. Use to join notes that you can't play legato.
5. Use to sustain bass under a treble passage.

6. Never use when a staccato effect is required.

7. Never use during rests. (They mean silence, remember?)

In a grand piano the soft pedal moves the whole keyboard action to one side so that the hammer strikes two strings (softer) instead of three strings (louder). It may be used with or without the damper pedal. Its effect is somewhat akin to the muting of strings. Learn to rely on your touch for soft playing and use the soft pedal for contrast.

Now we'd like you to consider two more "sharp" Key Signatures. You have learned the Key of C (no sharps and no flats). You've learned the Key of F (1 flat, B♭). You've learned the Key of G (1 sharp, F♯). You remember that the order of sharp keys goes up in fifths.

So play five notes up from G and you get D. The number 2 sharp key is the Key of D.

The Key Signature looks like this:

Plate 151

The minute you see this Key Signature you should instantly deduce the following:

There are two sharps in the Key Signature, F♯ and C♯.

The No. 2 sharp key is called D Major. (1 above the last sharp . . i.e. C to D).

The piece is written in the Key of D Major.

All the F's and all the C's regardless of their position on the piano or on the staves will be played as F♯ and C♯.

The Key of D Major means that all the notes in the piece will relate to each other in the same way as the notes in any other scale that you've learned.

The intervals between the notes are exactly the same as for the other Keys except that D is now Number 1.

Please go back for a moment and look at Plate 89. Read through the text concerning G Major. Now consider:

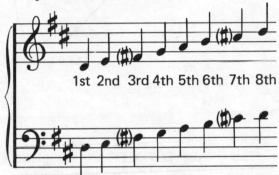

1st 2nd 3rd 4th 5th 6th 7th 8th

1st 2nd 3rd 4th 5th 6th 7th 8th

Plate 152

Therefore if we ask you to play a D Major 3rd you would play a D and an F♯. Practise finding and counting the intervals in the Key of D Major. Again try "thinking" in this new key. Play a C Major Triad, then a G Major Triad, then a D Major Triad. Educate your ears to the difference. As in the other keys:

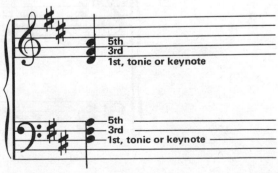

Plate 153

this represents the D Major Triad Chord on both staves. It is in the Tonic or D Position, meaning that the Tonic or Key Note, D, is at the bottom.

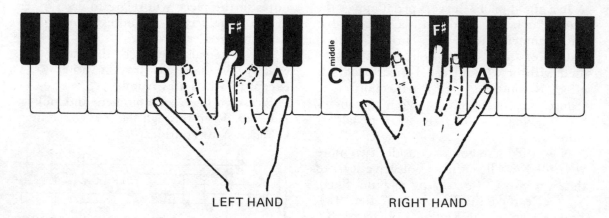

LEFT HAND   RIGHT HAND

Plate 154

This is the D POSITION. Compare it with the C, G, and F Positions. Practise it in exactly the same way. Play the notes, take your hands off the piano, look away, then try to play the chords quickly and accurately. Practise the first and second inversion. Now you can include the Scale of D Major along with its arpeggios in your regular practice.

You remember from Chapter Six that the Harmonic Minor of any Major scale is formed by flatting the third and the sixth by a semi-(half) tone.

Look again at the D Major Scale in Plate 152. If we were writing a piece in D Minor and kept the D Major Key Signature of two sharps we would have to naturalise every F sharp and Flat every B.

We would end up with this:

Plate 155

It is easier to give a piece written in the Key of D Minor the Key Signature of one flat so that we end up like this:

Plate 156

All this comes about because every Major Scale has what is called a Relative (related to—as in brother, sister) minor.

This can be confusing so don't dwell on it. If you never understand it your playing won't suffer. But consider the following very simple rules. We will illustrate them in the Key of C with which you are now thoroughly familiar.

1. Every Major Scale has a Relative Minor.
2. The Key Signature is the same for both.
3. The Relative Minor scale begins on the 6th of the Major Scale.
4. The Relative Minor is formed by raising the 7th one semi-(half) tone.

Plate 157

A Minor is the "Relative Minor" to C Major.

Now count five notes up from D and you reach A.

The Number Three Sharp Key is A Major.

The Key Signature looks like this:

Plate 158

The minute you see this Key Signature (as in all our previous examples) you should instantly deduce the following:

There are three sharps in the Key Signature, F♯, C♯ and G♯.

The Number 3 Sharp Key is A Major (1 above the last Sharp, i.e. G to A.

The piece is written in the Key of A Major.

All the F's, C's and G's will be played as F♯, C♯ and G♯.

The Key of A Major means that all the notes in the piece will relate to each other in the same way as the notes in the other scales you have learned.

So consider:

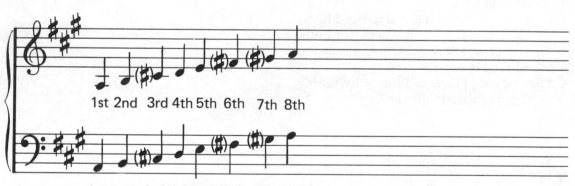

Plate 159

Therefore if we ask you to play an A Major Third you will play an A and a C♯. Practise finding and counting the intervals in the Key of A Major, exactly the way you did for the other scales. The A Major Position in the right hand is 1st finger on A, 3rd finger on C♯ and 5th finger on E. The A Major Position in the left hand is 5th finger on A, 3rd finger on C♯ and 1st finger on E.

Practise finding the A Major Position in exactly the same way as you did for the other Keys. Also practise the first and second inversions.

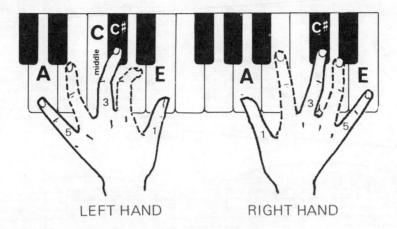

LEFT HAND   RIGHT HAND

Plate 160

Now let us talk about phrasing.

A sentence, in English, can be described as a group of words expressing a complete thought. The simplest possible sentence consists of a subject and a verb.

I eat.

This is actually a very good sentence in that it is neat, concise, clear and above all short. It is not, however, terribly interesting.

"If I eat too much rich food I gain weight," is a more interesting sentence and you will note that you cannot put a period anywhere within it. The thought is not complete until the very end.

You might think of phrasing in music as the intelligent grouping of musical sounds to make complete sense. There are "breathing spaces" in music just the way there are in speech. You can find the breaks or breathing spaces in any musical line by the simplest method of all. Sing it. Where you breathe naturally will be the end of a phrase. Phrases, like sentences, can end on either a strong beat or a weak one.

Sing "GOD SAVE THE QUEEN" out loud. You'll see that the first and second phrases end on a weak beat but that the third phrase ends on a strong one. Phrases in music are indicated thus:

Plate 161

a curved line written above or below the passage.

Study a few songs because the musical phrasing follows the punctuation of the words.

Phrasing is frequently very much a matter of personal taste as is interpretation. Two equally superb actors will play HAMLET differently. There is no "right" or "wrong" involved. If you're the emotional romantic type and want to "ham up" a piece that's your affair. Two superb pianists will frequently disagree about phrasing and again it is difficult to flatly say that one way is the "right" way.

Let us start off with something very very simple. Here is an old traditional French-Canadian Folk Song.

OLD FRENCH FOLK SONG

Plate 162

This is the way we suggest you practise this piece (and indeed all the others in this book). Attack it from two points of view.

1. Notation and Time

Obviously you must play the right notes and give each one its exact time value.

You observe, first of all, that the piece is written in the Key of G Major. Spend ten minutes practising your G Major Scale and Chords. Get yourself "thinking" in the Key of G Major. You then realise instantly that the interval (distance) between the Tonic G in Bar 1 and the B in Bar 2 is one third. You should be able to "feel" these intervals in your mind without touching the keyboard.

Now you observe that the piece is written in ¼ or Common Time. You realise that this Time Signature means there are four beats to each bar and that a quarter note or crotchet gets one beat. The direction "Moderato" means a moderate speed and the performance tempo is indicated as Mm 96 = ♩ . This means that each "tick" of your Metronome has the duration of a quarter note or crotchet. You know then that in Bar 1 each of the four crotchets will receive one beat. In Bar 2 each of the two half notes or minims will receive two beats. Bar 3 counts out exactly the same way as Bar 1. Bar 4 has a dotted half note or minim and you realise that the • after the note increases its duration by one half. So the dotted minim or half note in Bar 3 will receive three beats. You observe the quarter note or crotchet rest in Bar 4 so do not hold the dotted minim G for four beats instead of three. Without touching your piano count out the right hand all the way through using your Metronome. Then do the same thing with your left hand.

Next, without touching the keyboard, "tap" through the piece with your forefinger on top of your piano. Do this for the right hand first, then for the left. Then tap through the piece with both hands together.

Now play the right hand alone, still using your Metronome, making sure you are playing the right notes and giving each one its exact time value. Now do the same thing with the left. Try playing the right hand ten times alone, then the left hand ten times alone, then put them together. If you make mistakes slow down instantly. Set your Metronome at around 50. When you can play the piece correctly and without hesitation at 50, gradually speed it up until you can play it correctly at 96. When you are solidly confident of the right notes and time, begin to think about:

2. Interpretation and Style

Now with your Metronome still set at 96 = ♩ , play the right hand alone. Note that Bars 1 and 2 constitute a phrase or musical thought. Note also that Bars 3 and 4, although using different notes, repeat this phrase. You observe that the direction *p* for Piano means softly, so play the piece softly. Note the Crescendo beginning in Bar 9, holding through Bar 10 with a Diminuendo beginning in Bar 11 and ending in Bar 12. Bar 13 is marked *pp*, very softly, and should be half as loud as Bars 1 and 2.

Now observe the left hand. It consists entirely of quarter notes or crotchets, and constitutes an accompaniment of the melody played by the right hand. Since the melody is what should stand out, play your left hand with a softer tone than your right.

Now concern yourself with the pedalling as indicated. If there is the slightest degree of "blurring" of the notes your pedalling is wrong. Too little pedal is always preferable to too much. When you are thoroughly secure with this first piece move on to the second, "TWINKLE, TWINKLE LITTLE STAR". The melody is also French traditional in origin.

You may feel these little pieces are childish and you are quite right. But please don't try to run before you can walk. A Chopin Prelude is coming up next, and unless you thoroughly master these very easy pieces you will find it discouragingly difficult.

So concentrate on the following:

TWINKLE TWINKLE LITTLE STAR

Arr. Junkin/Ornadel

Plate 163

78

Use exactly the same practice methods on this second piece as you did on the first. Try singing the words and see how the sense in English matches the musical sense. When you can play both these little pieces perfectly and have them memorised take a deep breath and move on to your first really serious piece.

Frederic Chopin (1810-1849) was a Polish composer and pianist remembered both for his romantic life and his highly individual compositions for the piano. He wrote over two hundred Etudes, Nocturnes, Sonatas, Ballades, Preludes and Waltzes. His music is particularly notable for unusual and haunting harmonies and exquisite melodies.

PRELUDE

Chopin

Arr. Junkin/Ornadel

Plate 164

Use the same methods of practice as you did on the two earlier and much easier pieces. Attack the Prelude from two points of view:

1. Notation and Time

You observe first of all that it is written in the Key of A Major. Spend ten minutes practising your A Major Scale and Chords. Get yourself "thinking" in the Key of A Major and feeling the intervals in your mind.

Now observe that it is written in ¾ time which means there are three beats to each bar and that a quarter note (crotchet) gets one beat. The direction "Andantino" is a tempo slightly faster than "Andante" (moderately slow and distinct). The performance tempo is about 72 = ♩ on your Metronome but please start practising it with your Metronome set about as slowly as it will go, around 40 = ♩ . Without touching the piano keys count the piece through with your Metronome set in this position. Then "tap it" on the wood of your piano keeping strict time. Note that the first bar begins on the third beat. You are counting: 3/1.2.3./1.2.3. And etc. Get the rhythmic pattern very clearly established in your mind. Dah dahh de dah dah dahhhh.

When you can tap the right hand all the way through without hesitation observe the left hand.

It is a simpler rhythm . . an accompaniment really, of the right hand melody. Three quarter notes (crotchets) followed by a half note (minim) all the way through. Without touching the keyboard tap the left hand all the way through until you can do it without hesitation.

You now have a clear sense of the rhythmic picture of the piece.

Now with your Metronome still set at approximately 40 = ♩ play the right hand alone. Concentrate on giving each note its exact value and use the fingering indicated in the text. When you have played the right hand through ten times without hesitating on either time or notes start on the left hand.

Still with your Metronome set at 40 = ♩ play the left hand alone. When you have played the left hand ten times without hesitating on either time or notes:

Put the hands together.

When you have played the piece through hands together ten times without hesitating on either time or notes increase the tempo by moving your Metronome up to 60 = ♩ . If you find you are making mistakes slow down instantly. Gradually increase your tempo until you can play the piece through without hesitating on either time or notes at a tempo of 72 = ♩ . Be sure that the 16th notes (semiquavers) are played as such. Do NOT play:

Plate 165

2. Interpretation and Style

You observe the *p* for Piano meaning softly. Dolce means sweetly. So you are after a basic idea behind this Prelude that is soft and sweet. You can think of anything you like. If you want to think of a young boy being shy about telling a beautiful girl he likes her, fine. Pedal exactly as indicated. Down on beat one of bar 2 and up on beat two of bar 3. You have four phrases in the same rhythm repeating themselves up to beat two of bar 9. Try for some variety. Play phrases 1 and 2 slightly louder than phrases 3 and 4. Note that with phrase 5 you are starting to build up to the A Sharp chord at the end of phrase 6. Play gradually louder from the beginning of phrase 5 to the conclusion of phrase 6 so that you reach a natural climax.

Observe the slight crescendo and diminuendo in phrase 7. Observe the ritardando in phrase 8 .. most of which should occur on the last three chords in the phrase.

Practice for Lesson Seven

1. Scales as always. Concentrate on D Major and Minor and on A Major and Minor.
2. Continue to select pieces of music in ¾, ¾,. ¼, and ⅞ time and count the bars out correctly according to the Time Signature.
3. Work on the two traditional folk song pieces until you know them perfectly and then:
4. Work on the Chopin Prelude until you know it perfectly from memory.

An hour a day for three weeks and you should have this lesson pretty well under control.

And so endeth Lesson 7, PEDALLING AND PHRASING.

Lesson 8:
INTERPRETATION AND SHAPE

When you "interpret" a piece of music you should, hopefully, do more than merely perform it. Ideally you express as accurately as possible what the composer intended. The English word "interpretation" has the connotation of "explaining" or making clear some hidden meaning. An interpreter is sometimes a person who translates (explains and makes clear) one language into another. So think of interpretation as the act of getting the composer's ideas across as clearly as possible without overstating them. Sometimes these ideas are indicated fairly precisely by notation, expression marks, and phrasing marks. Even so, a great part of interpretation depends on your own personal taste. Hopefully this is based on knowledge, good judgment and restraint. We have all been either irritated or amused by the actor who "hams up" his part. By this we mean that he overdoes his emotions and gestures. This can sometimes effectively change a tragedy into a comedy. Restraint is probably the most important element in good interpretation but if you enjoy "hamming it up" there is no law that says this is wrong. Remember, too, that you can't interpret anything unless you understand it yourself.

So always try to decide on the "shape" of the piece. Is it a dance? If so, what sort of dance? Is it a fast dance or a slow one? Is it a waltz? If so, you must keep the rhythm absolutely constant for the benefit of the dancers. Is it a minuet, a mazurka, a tango? Or is it a march? If so, what sort of march? Is it a march of victory, joyous and triumphant? Or is it a march of defeat, sad and despairing? Or is it a funeral march or a religious procession?

Or is it a piano solo in the form of a song? If so, what sort of song? Is it a song of love and happiness? Or is it a song of death and despair? Is it a whimsical or funny song? Is it sung by a man or woman? The POLICEMAN'S SONG should be classified differently to THE SONG OF THE BROOK.

Is the piece meant to express any sort of idea? A lullaby, for example, suggests that a child is being put to sleep. You must not put him to sleep with boredom and you must not sing (play) so loudly that the youngster is kept awake.

Is there any distinctive thought of movement behind the piece? The ROLLER COASTER should be classified differently to THE SPINNING WHEEL. Or is there any thought of nationalism behind the piece such as you encounter in Liszt's HUNGARIAN RHAPSODIES?

Is there any distinctive "sound" behind the piece? THE BELL SONG is rather different to the BLACKSMITH'S SONG. Is there any sort of activity involved? THE GONDOLIER'S SONG will give a different impression to THE JUGGLER'S SONG. "STROLLING ALONG" has a different quality to "DANCE OF THE WITCHES".

In this lesson you will learn THE CRADLE SONG by Brahms and you should instantly understand "the shape" from the title. Almost certainly it is being sung by a mother to her child and obviously the child is in a cradle which is meant for sleeping in. Before we go on with this and some new Key Signatures, here are:

A few facts and definitions

FERMATA. (Italian). The sign ⌒ which directs that a note or rest is to be held for slightly longer than its time value indicates. The Italian is pretentious. Call it a "hold".

FLAMENCO. A type of music from Andalusia in Spain that is thought to date from the early 19th Century. Sometimes it accompanies dancers but can consist of singing with guitar accompaniment assisted by castanets to punctuate the rhythm. The mood ranges from sad and plaintive to fiery and brilliant.

SONATA. An important form of instrumental music for either a keyboard instrument or others, usually consisting of three sections or movements in contrasting tempo, i.e. fast-slow-fast. The first and third movements are usually in the same key while the second is usually in a different key.

TRILL. One of the most frequently used musical ornaments. It consists of the rapid alternation of a note with the note a half or whole tone above it. The exact number of notes played depends on your dexterity and on the tempo.

Written

Played

Plate 166

OPUS. From the Latin "work". Used with a number it indicates either the order of the composer's works or the order in which they were published. Opus 1 is presumably the composer's first work. A single Opus may include one or several compositions; in the latter case the pieces are usually related. There are twelve preludes in Chopin's Opus 10. They are referred to individually as Opus 10, No. 1, No. 2, etc.

Please take a moment now to go back to Lesson Six and briefly review your No. 1 Flat Key of F Major.

The order of Flat Keys goes down in 5ths and five down from F brings you to B Flat.

The Key Signature looks like this:

Plate 167

The minute you see this Key Signature you should instantly deduce the following:

There are two flats in the Key Signature, B♭ and E♭.

The No. 2 Flat Key is B♭ Major.

The piece is written in the Key of B Flat Major.

You learned in Lesson Seven that every Major Scale has a relative Minor. The Relative Minor begins on the 6th of the Major Scale so the piece could also be written in the Key of G Minor. (G is the 6th of B♭ Major).

The Key of B♭ Major or G Minor means that all the B's and all the E's, regardless of their position on the staves or piano are played as B♭ and E♭.

Again the distances between the notes are exactly the same as for the other Scales you have learned.

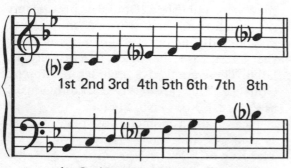

1st 2nd 3rd 4th 5th 6th 7th 8th

1st 2nd 3rd 4th 5th 6th 7th 8th

Plate 168

Therefore if we ask you to play a B Flat Major 3rd you would play B Flat and a D. In the Key of B Flat Major B♭ is always 1, C is 2, D is 3, etc. Again practise finding and counting your intervals in the Key of B Flat Major.

Notice, in the back of the book, that because the Scale of B Flat Major begins on a black note that the fingering is different. As before you know that:

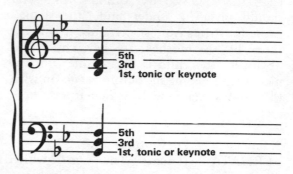

Plate 169

represents the B Flat Major Triad Chord on both staves. It is in the Tonic position, meaning that the tonic or Key Note B♭ is at the bottom.

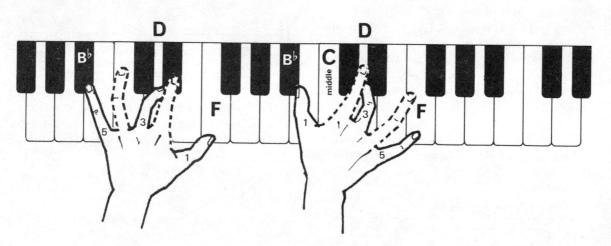

Plate 170

This is the B Flat Major Position. Compare it with the F Position. Again practise it the same way, taking your hands off the piano, looking away, then finding the chords with both hands as quickly and accurately as possible.

We will not go into this detail for the remaining Key Signatures. Learn one new one every two weeks, in the same way you learned the others. The Scales and Arpeggios for all Key Signatures are at the back of this book.

Counting five down from B Flat you arrive at E Flat. The Key Signature looks like this:

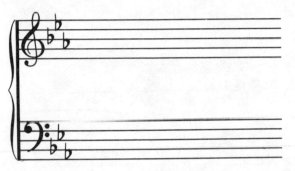

Plate 171

E Flat Major is the Number 3 Flat Key. Three Flats, B♭ , E♭ and A♭ .

Counting five down from E Flat you arrive at A Flat. The Key Signature looks like this:

Plate 172

A Flat Major is the Number 4 Flat Key. Four Flats. B♭ , E♭ , A♭ and D♭ .

Counting five down from A Flat you arrive at D Flat. The Key Signature looks like this:

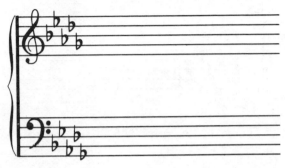

Plate 173

D Flat Major is the Number 5 Flat Key. Five Flats. B♭ , E♭ , A♭ , D♭ and G♭ .

You have already learned the Keys of C. G. D. and A Major. Counting five up from A you arrive at E. Its Key Signature looks like this:

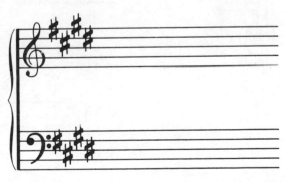

Plate 174

E Major is the Number 4 Sharp Key. Four Sharps. F♯ , C♯ , G♯ and D♯ .

Counting five up from E you arrive at B. Its Key Signature looks like this:

Plate 175

B Major is the Number 5 Sharp Key. Five Sharps, F♯, C♯, G♯, D♯, and A♯.

Now let us move on to another piece, this one by Johannes Brahms. He was one of the outstanding figures in Nineteenth Century music and was born in Hamburg in 1833. In 1863 he settled in Vienna which remained his permanent home until his death in 1897. He composed in every musical form except opera. His major orchestral works include four symphonies, two piano concertos (both gorgeous and you'd love them) and one violin concerto. He wrote a very large number of pieces for the piano as well as hundreds of songs some of which rank among the finest ever written.

Here is his Cradle Song.

CRADLE SONG
Johannes Brahms (1833-1897)

Arr. Junkin/Ornadel

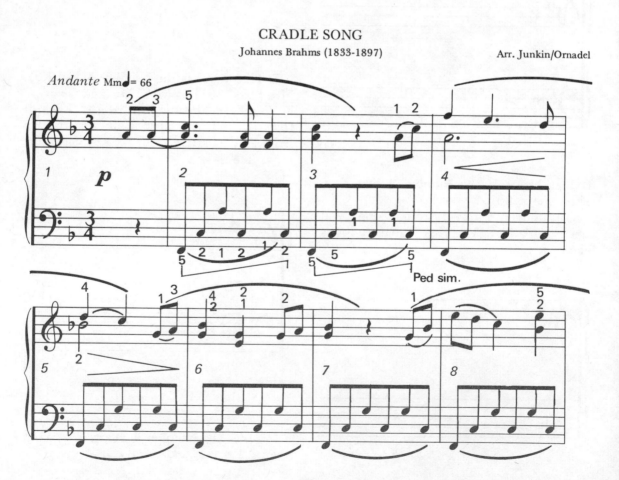

Plate 176

We will again go into the detailed practice methods so that eventually you can learn to apply them automatically to every piece you learn. We will approach it from two points of view:

1. Notation and Time

You observe, first of all, that the piece is written in the Key of F Major. Spend ten minutes practising your F Major Scales and Chords so that you are "thinking" in the Key of F Major and "feeling" the intervals.

Next you see that the piece is written in $\frac{3}{4}$ time which means there are three beats to each bar and that a quarter note or crotchet gets one beat. The direction Andante means Moderately Slow and distinct, and the performance tempo is indicated by a Metronome marking of 66. You observe that the piece *starts* on the third beat of the Bar. Look at the last bar and you will see that it contains only two beats. So the first two eighth notes or quavers begin with the count 3. The first dotted quarter note or crotchet in Bar 2 is played on the count of 1. In other words you are counting: 3/1.2.3./1.2.3./and etc.

Without touching the keyboard "tap" through the piece with your forefinger on top of the piano. Note that in Bar 2 you are concerned with a dotted quarter note or crotchet so avoid the temptation to play these notes as three quarter notes or crotchets.

Observe in Bar 4 that the dotted half note or minim is held for a count of three through the entire bar. The same thing occurs again in Bar 12.

Now play the right hand alone, still using your Metronome set at 66. Make sure you are playing the right notes and giving each one its exact time value.

Now do the same thing with the left hand. Observe that the pattern in the left hand is the same from Bar 2 to the end of Bar 15. Observe that in Bars 2, 3 and 4 the left hand notes are identical. They change in Bar 5, but Bars 5, 6, 7 and 8 are identical. If you find the fingering in Bar 2: 5-2-1-2-1-2 too difficult, or if you have very small hands, use the fingering in Bar 3: 5-5-1-5-1-5. The fingering in Bar 2 is preferable if you can manage it. It will give you a smoother rhythm and a nicer legato. When you can play the left hand through evenly and smoothly with your Metronome at 66—try playing both hands together. If you make too many mistakes slow down instantly. Set your Metronome as slow as it will go and gradually increase your speed until you reach 66. When you are solidly confident of the right notes and time, begin to think about:

2. Interpretation and Style

First of all you notice the name, "CRADLE SONG". As we said earlier, this must mean a song sung by a mother to a child in a cradle. There are words written to this which being, "Lullaby . . and goodnight". So immediately you are going to think of a mother who loves her baby tenderly. You should also deduce that the repetitive left hand pattern is suggestive of a cradle rocking regularly back and forth. Use the marked pedalling and think of Bar 2 as one complete rock and forth of the cradle. Apply this to all of the bars with the exception of Bar 16 where the child is (presumably) asleep and the cradle stops rocking through inertia. This is what the ritard (rit) means.

You observe the piece is to be played *p* for Piano, softly. It drifts away at the end to *pp* for Pianissimo, *very* softly. Observe the *small* crescendoes in Bars 4 and 12. The diminuendoes in Bars 5 and 13 must match these. The diminuendo in Bar 15 is to drift right off to *pp* pianissimo (sleep) in Bar 17. Note that the first phrase ending in the middle of Bar 3 is a complete musical thought.

Aim for smoothness and tenderness of touch, gentleness and softness. A Cradle Song must be restful, peaceful and comforting. And if you play Bars 1 through 15 as softly as you can—you will be unable to play any softer for Bars 16 and 17. As you remember, loudness and softness are relative.

Now let us move on to a little Tchaikovsky piece.

Peter Ilich Tchaikovsky was born in Russia in 1840. He began his career as a government clerk and did not turn seriously to music until he was twenty. Outstanding among his many works, notable especially for their exquisite melodies, are his Symphonies 4, 5 and 6. He wrote piano and violin concertos, the operas Eugene Onegin and The Queen of Spades, both still widely performed. He is perhaps best known for the music he wrote for ballets, Swan Lake, Sleeping Beauty and The Nutcracker.

Now consider his Serenade for Strings.

SERENADE FOR STRINGS

Tchaikovsky

Arr. Junkin/Ornadel

Valse Allegro Mm♩= 132
Sweetly and gracefully

Plate 177

We will delineate your practice methods in less detail since by now you should be getting the general idea. As before you attack the piece from two points of view:

1. Notation and Time

You observe the Key Signature as 1 ♯ or G Major. Again, you practise your G Major Scales and Chords before beginning the piece. But notice that in Bar 2 the chords are the G Major Triad 2nd Inversion, the Tonic (G) in the second position from the top. This chord occurs frequently throughout the piece and is an example of why you must be able to find and play chords automatically.

You notice the marking Valse Allegro. A waltz at a fairly fast tempo. Obviously it must not be faster than human feet can move unless you imagine it being danced by a centipede. A Metronome mark of 132 is indicated. Since it is a "dance" you will be very careful in the liberties you take with strict time. When you tap the right hand out with your finger on top of the piano, you should sense the slight emphasis on the first beat of every bar. ONE, two, three, ONE, two, three. This emphasis gives the rhythm a swinging, lilting feel. You observe that Bar 1 begins on the second beat. So you are counting 2.3./1.2.3/1.2.3./ and etc.

The small notes in Bars 6, 10, 14 and 18 are called Grace Notes. A Grace Note is played very quickly just before the main note, and thus gives it an added accent. Its time value is not counted in the bar because it is borrowed from the duration of the note either immediately before or immediately after it. Grace notes do *not* affect your count. Do *not* regard them as two sixteenth notes or semiquavers.

As usual tap out the right hand with your forefinger on top of your piano with your Metronome set at 132.

Now tap out the left hand. It is straight 1.2.3. rhythm with the accent on the first beat of every bar. Be sure you hold the dotted half notes or minims in Bars 7, 10, 11, 12, 13, 14, 15, 16, 17, 18, 19 and 20 for three full beats. In Bars 2 to 9 make sure you do *not* play the quarter notes or crotchets as though they were dotted half notes or minims.

Now practise hands separately with your Metronome set at about 90. Then put both hands together and gradually increase your tempo to a Metronome mark of 132.

Be careful not to play the right hand eighth notes or quavers in Bars 4, 7, 11, 12, 15, 16 and 17 as quarter notes or crotchets. If you fail to observe the eighth note or quaver rest in these bars you "rob" the rhythm of some of its attractive lilt. When you are solidly confident of the right notes and time, begin to think about:

2. Interpretation and Style

You remember our definition of Serenade as a love song sung during the evening below the girl's (usually bedroom) window. You are in some conflict here with the term Waltz. So think of the piece as a song being sung in Waltz time by violins. This will allow you to take a little bit more liberty with the Time.

You are admonished to play the piece sweetly and gracefully. These are terms which everyone will interpret differently. Observe the expression marks exactly and slightly accent the first beat of every bar particularly in the left hand. This will help you achieve the lilting waltz quality that the piece demands.

Now let us move on to the SOLDIER'S MARCH by Robert Schumann.

Schumann was born in 1810 in Zwickau, Germany. A career as a concert pianist was prevented by a permanent hand injury which he suffered in 1832 through overzealous exercising of his fingers. He then turned exclusively to composition, writing exclusively for the piano until 1840. Then his wife, Clara, herself a pianist of the first rank, encouraged him to try his hand at songs. In 1840 he wrote over a hundred of them and these contain some of his finest works. He has also composed symphonies, string quartets and other chamber music.

SOLDIER'S MARCH
R. Schumann (1810-1856)

Arr. Junkin/Ornadel

Tempo di Marcia Mm♩= 120

Plate 178

What you have learned about practising can now be applied to any piece of music you care to attempt. Again, you observe the Key and Time Signatures. Be sure that you do not play the eighth notes or quavers as staccato. They are not written:

Plate 179

Each eighth note or quaver gets exactly a half beat and each must be played for its full time value. Emphasise the first beat in each bar slightly. ONE, two, ONE, two. Keep very strict time since, as you observe from the title, it is a piece for soldiers to march to. Observe the accent marks exactly as written: — over or under a note suggests

an added emphasis that is slightly less than $>$.

Observe that the two bars beginning at Letter A are identical in structure with the two bars beginning at Letter B, and that A is marked *f* and B is marked *mf*. Observe this as it gives the piece colour and variety. Try always to avoid monotony in your playing.

We come now to the final piece in the book, Beethoven's MINUET IN G.

Ludwig van Beethoven (1770-1827) was a German composer whose nine symphonies mark him as perhaps the outstanding architect of Western music. His output was enormous and includes piano concertos, violin concertos, and no less than thirty-two piano sonatas. His compositions, in virtually every form, bridge the classic and romantic periods of musical history.

MINUET IN G

Beethoven

Arr. Junkin/Ornadel

Plate 180

Once again you approach this piece from the two standpoints of Notation and Time, and Interpretation and Style. Practise it exactly as you did the previous pieces. By now you should realise that everything demanded of the performer is actually there in the music. You will not always see it unless you look for it carefully. Avoid the fault of playing the thirds as three groups of eighth notes or quavers when they are written as dotted eighth notes or quavers with sixteenth notes or semi-quavers. Observe the large number of G Major 3rds and 5ths. They occur in almost every bar and again illustrate how important it is that you learn your chords and intervals until finding and playing them becomes automatic. There should be the faintest emphasis on the first beat of each bar, ONE-two-three, ONE-two-three, but not as marked as in a Waltz. The aimed-for style is one of grace, delicacy and restraint. This is far from being a swinging dance. Instead imagine a very beautiful lady dancing it at the court of Louis XIV.

We are now at the end of this book and there are many aspects of pianism which we have not even mentioned let alone explored in detail. Touch is one; technique is another. Technique might be defined as the ability to play the right notes at the correct tempo with the chosen quantity and quality of tone. Obviously this definition is vastly over-simplified which is why hundreds of books have been written on the subject. You may want to read some of them and we hope you do. Some of the world's greatest pianists never practise finger exercises or scales but content themselves with mastering technical problems as they arise. We do not recommend this approach for the beginner.

Scale practice is essential. Work on them along the lines we have suggested and use the Metronome markings given in the section on Scales. Incorporate every possible attack and dynamic variation that you can think of, staccato, legato and accent. Practise every shade of piano and forte, even the most minute inflections. Pay attention that you are not always playing *ff* or *ppp*. Develop variety in a medium tone too. Every forte passage does not have to sound like an explosion. Above all listen for smoothness and exact time values.

We will leave you with a few "do's", "don'ts" and suggestions.

If you are interested buy some books of finger exercises and a book on piano technique.

If you really *listen* to your playing you can teach yourself a great deal. Sometimes you only *think* you are doing what you intend to do and a tape recorder can be embarrassingly revelatory.

If you bring the right mental attitude to your practising it is impossible for you not to enjoy it. Take one step at a time. As we suggested at the beginning you are never going to give a piano recital at the Festival Hall. But you can, if you want to, derive enormous pleasure from music.

Try to train yourself to read music as quickly as you read English. Get into the habit of reading a bar ahead so you know what is coming and are prepared for it.

It is said that Liszt had a sign over his piano for the edification of his pupils which read: "Think ten times and play once." You will not, necessarily, improve a passage by playing it a dozen times. You must know *why* you are repeating it and what you want to accomplish. By thinking first you may achieve the desired effect after four playings thus eliminating eight needless repetitions.

Try to plan your practice. If you have only one hour at your disposal take the first three minutes to plan the remaining fifty-seven.

If you decide to move on to better and bigger things, and we hope you will, learn all you can about the "style" of the composer. Don't play Bach like Chopin and both of them like John Brown.

Be careful of your Metronome. It is your best friend. Always use it when practising scales and when you are learning a new piece. You must *know* your time perfectly before you can take liberties with it.

Don't just *look* at a piece of music. *Study* it! Notice every little dot, tie, slur, rest or accent.

Use your imagination. *Think* about your beautiful French lady dancing the MINUET IN G. *Think* about the platoon keeping time to your SOLDIER'S MARCH. Give yourself mental images, waves, clouds, wind blowing over wild flowers.

Don't regard indicated fingering as irrevocable. Choose the fingering that is easiest and most comfortable for your hands.

Be relaxed in your approach, be diligent in your practice, don't try to run before you can walk, don't be ashamed of being an amateur, don't be impatient and above all, don't be discouraged too easily.

Good luck, enjoy yourselves and remember . . . The Piano Can Be Fun!

Glossary of Terms

Middle C	The name of the first degree or keynote of the natural scale of C situated in the middle of the piano keyboard. Its tone is produced by strings vibrating at 256 cycles per second.
Stave	The lines and spaces on which music is written.
Leger Lines	Short lines (and spaces) added below or above a stave when notes occur that are too high or too low to be accommodated within the stave itself.
Semi-tone	A half tone. The smallest interval used in normal European music.
Whole tone	Two consecutive semi-tones.
Octave	The distance, up or down, between two tonic or Key notes in any Major or Minor Scale.
Scale	See Page 15.
Harmonic Minor	See Page 64.
Relative Minor	See Page 73.
Contrary Motion	The playing of scales in opposite directions with both hands. i.e. the right hand going up and the left hand going down and vice versa.
Chromatic Scale	A scale consisting of semi-tones only.
Arpeggio	A chord "spread" i.e. the notes heard one after the other from the bottom upwards. Or the use of notes of a chord in rapid succession instead of simultaneously.
Notation	Notes placed on the lines and spaces of a stave.
Concert Pitch	The tuning of the A above Middle C to 440 vibrations per second.
Absolute Pitch	The ability to recognise by ear alone a note in the scale without reference to any previous note.
Clef	A character placed on a stave to indicate the name and pitch of the notes on the stave. Hence, Treble Clef 𝄞 and Bass Clef 𝄢
Bar	The space between one bar line and the next.
Sight-read	The ability to play a piece of unknown music at sight with accuracy as to notes and time.

Chord	Any combination of notes simultaneously played. For example, a triad chord is a chord consisting of three notes played together.
Interval	The distance and difference in pitch between any two notes.
Inversion	(of a chord) The placing of the Keynote of the chord in another position than the bottom note. For example, a C Major Triad is made up of C. E. G. The first inversion would be E. G. C. The second inversion would be G. C. E.
Tonic	The Keynote from which the key takes its name, as Key of C. C is the Tonic.
Bar Line	The vertical line separating the bars.
Key Signature	An indication at the beginning of a composition of the Key in which the piece is written, e.g. two flats, one sharp, etc.
Semi-breve	Whole note. In ¼ or Common Time a semi-breve gets four beats.
Minim	Half note, half value of a semi-breve.
Crotchet	Quarter note, half the value of a minim.
Quaver	Eighth note, half the value of a quarter note.
Semi-quaver	Sixteenth note, half the value of an eighth note.
Demi-semi-quaver	Thirty-second note, half the value of a sixteenth note.
Dotted notes	A dot after any note prolongs its count for one half of its original time value. Thus, a dotted quarter note is held for the time value of a quarter note and an eighth note.
Tied notes	A curved line placed over or under a note and its repetition to show that the two should be played as one unbroken note.
Slur	A curved line over or under notes indicating they are to be played smoothly. In string music they are to be played in one movement of the bow.
Grace Note	A musical embellishment not usually given time value.
Metronome	An instrument for marking the time by means of a graduated inverted pendulum with a sliding weight which can be regulated.
Common Time	The most frequent time signature. It is indicated by **C** or ¼ meaning that there are four beats to a bar and a crotchet or quarter note gets one beat.
Triplet	Three notes joined together to be played in the time allotted to two in the Time Signature.
Rhythm	Everything in music relating to time as distinct from pitch.
Rest	A period of silence in a musical composition, given the same time value as its related note. Thus there are distinctive signs for whole note rests, half note or minim rests, etc.
Piano	Indicated by *p* . Means soft.
Pianissimo	Indicated by *pp*. Means very soft.

Forte	Indicated by f. Means loud.
Fortissimo	Indicated by ff. Means very loud.
Concerto	A musical composition for a solo instrument accompanied by an orchestra, usually in three movements.
Symphony	Music played by a number of orchestral performers, usually in four movements.
Fermata	A sign written over a note or rest indicating a pause or hold, written thus: ⌒
Sonata	An instrumental composition, see Page 83.
Trill	The repetition of two notes in rapid succession, the most important musical "ornament".
Opus	From the Latin "work". Usually written Op. followed by a number, indicating the order in which a composer's works were published.
Anthem	A musical composition for a church choir, on a religious theme, accompanied by the organ and frequently incorporating passages for one or more solo voices.
Aria	A solo vocal passage usually, but not always, from an opera.
Cantata	A work for several solo voices, choir, etc., sung without scenery or acting, usually on a religious theme.
Oratorio	A work on a religious theme for solo vocalists, chorus and orchestra for either concert or church performance, usually without scenery, costumes or action.
Movement	A section of a larger work, complete in itself, but so designed as to combine effectively with other movements into a larger composition. E.g. movements of a concerto or symphony.
Etude	Study written to improve the technique of the instrumentalist.
Prelude	A piece of music composed to be played before any other piece of music or play, ceremony, etc.
Waltz	A dance in three/four time with a strong accent on the first beat.
Minuet	A dance in three/four time with an unhurried tempo.
Flamenco	Type of melody popular in Andalusia, used in both song and dance; the term is especially applied to gypsy music.
Ballade	Name given by Chopin to a long dramatic type of piano piece, the musical equivalent of a stirring poetical ballad of the heroic type.
Serenade	Music sung and played usually at night below a lady's window.
Barcarolle	A boat song or an instrumental composition with a steady rhythm like that of oarsmen.
Rhapsody	An instrumental composition enthusiastic in character but of indefinite form.
Impromptu	An instrumental composition of a character suggesting improvisation.

Tarantella	A dance which takes its name from Taranto, Italy, or from a poisonous spider, Tarantula, common there, the rapid dance being a cure for the disease caused by the poisonous bite.
Crescendo	Gradually getting louder, indicated in music by
Diminuendo	Gradually getting softer, indicated by
Legato	Performed with a smooth connection between the notes.
Staccato	The opposite of legato, performed with each note clearly detached and sharp. Indicated by a dot over or under the note.
Tempo	Time at which composition should be played.
Ritard	Or ritardando, gradually slowing down, written rit.
Accelerando	Gradually faster, written accel.
Prestissimo	Very quickly. Mm. 208
Presto	Quickly. Mm. 184
Vivace	Played in lively fashion, vivaciously. Mm. 160
Allegro	Merry, quick, lively, bright. Mm. 132
Animato	Played in animated fashion. Mm. 120
Allegretto	Lively, but not as fast as allegro. Mm. 108
Moderato	At a moderate speed. Mm. 88
Andante	Smoothly flowing, not too quickly. Mm. 66
Andantino	A little faster than andante. Mm. 89
Lento	Slowly. Mm. 56
Adagio	Slowly and easily. Mm. 52
Largo	Very slow and dignified. Mm. 46
Grave	With slow speed and solemnity, as a Funeral March. Mm. 40.

BRAHMS, Johannes, b. Hamburg 1833, d. Vienna 1897.

TCHAIKOVSKY, Peter Ilich, b. Kamsko-Votinsk, 1840, d. St. Petersburg 1893.

SCHUMANN, Robert Alexander, b. Zwickau, Saxony, 1810, d. in mental asylum nr. Bonn, 1856.

BEETHOVEN, Ludwig van, b. Bonn 1770, d. Vienna 1827.

LISZT, Franz, b. Raiding, Hungary, 1811, d. Bayreuth 1886.

CHOPIN, Frederic Francois, b. Zelazowa Wola, Poland, 1810, d. Paris 1849.

Scales and Arpeggios

Tempo:

STEP 1:	Practise scales hands separately with a MM ♪ = 56
STEP 2:	Increase the tempo hands separately gradually until you are playing the scales smoothly and accurately at a MM ♩ = 92
STEP 3:	Practise scales hands together with a MM ♩ = 56
STEP 4:	Increase the tempo hands together gradually until you are playing the scales smoothly and accurately at MM ♩ = 92
STEP 5:	Then attempt a MM of ♩ = 112.

Scale of C

Major　　　　　　　　　　　　　　Harmonic Minor

Scale of G

Major　　　　　　　　　　　　　　Harmonic Minor

Scale of F

Major   Harmonic Minor

Scale of D

Major   Harmonic Minor

Scale of B♭

Major   Harmonic Minor

Scale of A

Major   Harmonic Minor

Scale of E♭

Major · Harmonic Minor

Scale of E

Major · Harmonic Minor

Scale of A♭

Major · Harmonic Minor

Scale of B

Major · Harmonic Minor

Scale of D♭

Major   Harmonic Minor

Scale of F♯

Major   Harmonic Minor

Arpeggio of C

Major   Minor

Arpeggio of G

Major   Minor

Arpeggio of F

Major

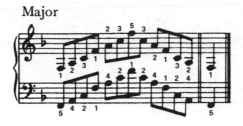

Minor

Arpeggio of D

Major

Minor

Arpeggio of B♭

Major

Minor

Arpeggio of A

Major

Minor

Arpeggio of E♭

Major

Minor

Arpeggio of E

Major

Minor

Arpeggio of A♭

Major

Minor

Arpeggio of B

Major

Minor

Arpeggio of D♭

Major

Minor

Arpeggio of F♯

Major

Minor